CHAPTER ONE

MORE IN YOU

DAWN FRANCIS

PRELUDE

As a child, I felt invincible, as many children do. But then you grow up and realize how small you are and how big the world is. The emotional weight of being and remaining strong can be overbearing. I remember countless times in ministry people telling me that I was strong. I hated hearing that because most of the comments came when I felt like I was weak. Although I was an adult at times, I still felt weak, educated but vulnerable, smart, gifted, and talented, but weak. When people said, "Girl, you are strong," that comment always came when I was struggling through a challenge. Why? I know with strength comes challenges and times of growth. How is this done?

Ephesians 6:10. Be Strong in the Lord and the Power of His Might....

Growing up as a pastor's kid gave me a ministry perspective that many may not have had. My parents gave so much of themselves in ministry. They taught me to fear God and keep His commandments. Their love for

God and ministry framed my life and love for God and ministry.

...

My mom was an incredible woman of faith. She taught and mentored women without a thought of her sacrifice of time. She would call my dad, Brother Williams, which today may seem odd but cute. She always showed him the utmost respect. The only time I heard her call him Al was when only family was around. Like clockwork, mom always had his meals on the table in a timely manner, knowing that with ministry, his work was never really over. She worked and took care of her husband and eight children like it was nothing and it seemed effortless as we all watched her become our champion mom. I can't even imagine how anyone could do this today. Her incredible strength was instilled in all of her children and blessed the many lives that she touched in ministry as the First Lady of her church.

Storytelling is a gift and daddy was an excellent storyteller. Mom loved his stories and always encouraged us as children to listen and pay attention to the meaning deep within the story. My dad, the late Bishop Alpheus Williams, used to tell a story in ministry about a man that worked so hard and walked home after work because he didn't have a car. One day, as he walked down the street heading home, he felt so tired, and his exhaustion overwhelmed him. Finally, he felt so tired that he couldn't go any further.

He said, "I can't take not one more step."

He saw a tree that gave him a little shade; he walked slowly up to the tree, lowered himself down, and leaned up against the tree. He laid his head back and right into a hornet's nest. Witnesses said they saw that same man, who said he couldn't go any further, running top speed down the street. I remember dad sharing that story and saying how there's more in us than we know. That was a message on strength. The gentleman discovered he was in fact capable of going many more steps forward.

Likewise, I noticed times when mom seemed to be doing so many things that I wondered how on earth she kept going. Raising eight children, tending to the ministry of the church, and working full time along with being a community servant wasn't easy. But mom never gave up. I hope that when read, you will indeed discover strength on the inside of you and that you realize that God has already given you all that you need.

I guess, in many ways, my mom was like that man. She always found the will and energy to go beyond her own tiredness and meet the needs of her family and church members. Mom influenced everyone around her by her gentleness, her courage, and stamina. The mothers in the church looked to her for guidance and words of encouragement. My mom was a comforter to so many people. The young ladies often were afraid as they also knew that she had the gift of discernment and would call them out to encourage them to do what was right.

I remember growing up in the church; I used to go to many funerals and sing. Whether I knew the deceased or not, I just wanted to bring whatever comfort that I could to the family; so, I rarely ever said no if a request came. I saw the pain and grief, but I didn't quite understand it. I was able to separate myself from the pain that I did not understand. I did not understand it because I had never lost a close family member.

I remember sitting with a friend of mine with her mother in the hospital. I was so young, not fully understanding the magnitude of losing a mother or being there with her for support. But this would all change when it was my turn. I would experience a barrage of loss, so extreme that I would need supernatural strength and intervention to make it through.

I lost my mom and dad within three months of each other when I was in my 20's. I lost my dad in August and my mom in October. Two weeks later, I lost my aunt who was my godmother. It seemed like one blow after the next. Such intense pain and anger along with grief raged through my soul, body, and mind. I thought to myself, how on earth could this be happening? Where is God in all of this? How could such devoted servants, as mom and dad, suffer such sudden loss? How could our family be torn apart so suddenly, leaving us eight children to go on without them? My parents had many more years to live and give Him glory. My mom was not sick, and I had no idea that it would happen so quickly. I just felt that there was no way that God would allow such a thing to occur. But it did happen. My family and I were devastated! We made every attempt to pull closer together and to rely on God to carry us through.

For someone who has never lost a close loved one, the challenge to relate to the grieving individual is real. There is very little the person can relate to no matter how much they may want to. They can be there, listen, pray, and encourage, but it is nearly impossible to understand this grief fully.

It's incredible to me how God uses our grief and life experiences to help others. Since the death of my parents, I have counseled and shared with countless families and individuals who too have lost their parents and loved ones. When I counsel, I must clarify that I pointed them in the direction of a professional counselor, listened to their cries, held them in my arms to allow the tears to flow, and was there when needed.

Grief counseling is a blessing to anyone going through a loss. My family members sought counseling, as did I after almost wrecking myself trying to act strong when I really needed shoulders to lean on. I used to put on a facade and say, "I am fine," but after a while, I couldn't handle it on my own. I am so thankful for the support that I received to become whole again. The stages of grief are real, and we all benefit from getting the support we need whether professional, ministerial, or friendship relationships. Pastoral counseling is also beneficial. Quite often my mom would offer spiritual direction through God's word to many people who came to her.

As the word of God says, we are our brother's keeper. We don't go through the things that we go through in life just for ourselves. We go through challenges to learn lessons for growth, walk-in victory, triumph, and conquer all that comes our way. It's about helping others as they go through different seasons of life. We go through life's hurdles, not just to learn lessons but so that we can sow good seeds into good ground.

Ephesians 6:10: Be Strong in the Lord and the Power of His Might.

PRAYER

Father God I pray for each person who is facing life challenges today. Thank you for strength and grace through every trial. Thank you that we hear your voice, and we follow after no one but you. Lord thank you for the strength to endure and to move forward. Help us to know that you have equipped and qualified us to do all that you have placed in our hearts to accomplish. In You we can do more. In Jesus' Name. Amen!

CHAPTER TWO

LOVE FOUND ME

PAULINE REID

PRELUDE

The best example of unconditional love that I grew up watching was my mom and dad. They were a couple that I saw and learned from. I saw the full definition of love in the way they treated each other. There were times in which I knew there were challenges, but never once did I hear my dad raise his voice or observe my mother disrespect him. Their union brought forth a family of eight children in which every one of us became a living example of their love. They taught us to love and respect each other and to love God and to keep His commandments.

...

I grew up playing the Alto horn and the French horn in school. I always had a love for music and harmonies. I performed in band both at school and at church. It's amazing how music played such a huge role in my life and in shaping the person that I am today. Singing was something that our family engaged in on a regular basis. I remember training my younger sisters to sing and mimic riffs and runs until they reached near perfection. It was fun and became second nature to each of us. Music, singing, and serving God was a part of our everyday lives.

I started directing the choir as a teen in my father's church. My dad had a passion for music, and we all learned to play various instruments. He had grown up as a young man playing in the famous Bahama Brass Band, a well-known band even today. That's all we knew and were taught to use our talents for the glory of God. Although I developed a passion for music and singing, my gift and anointing were for directing and leading the choir.

I can recall a moment during a program when our choir was up next to perform. As I stood up with the choir to take the stand, I felt the eyes of the people on us with great expectations.

The Choir was well-rehearsed, polished, confident but not arrogant. We were definitely an anointed Choir. That's not a brag, just a praise. We weren't an audition Choir, where everyone was able to sing and hold their parts. We had a small church choir. We allowed people to join whether or not they could sing well. As long as you were a Christian and love to sing, we worked with you. Trust me, we worked hard, but we really enjoyed the rehearsal time and fellowship together. I was a perfectionist, which required a great deal of work. I also took my task as a director seriously, yet I enjoyed having a good time or laughter.

When the music started, I stood before the choir, with excitement and great anticipation, expecting God to use us greatly so we could be a source of spiritual blessings, enjoyment, and inspiration. As I lifted my hands, the choir stood there with their eyes fastened on me, ready for my next move. Sometimes I felt as if they were an instrument that I was playing. I tried to pull out of them all that I could and what they were capable of giving. I wasn't too concerned about what I looked like while directing but more about how they sounded. I was also concerned about how much of a blessing they would be.

As they sang and the anointing flowed, I imagined gracefully pulling the notes out of each voice as if they were an orchestra. Every directive move I made, they responded likewise. It wasn't for a show as some would think, but I demanded a response with their sound or action.

I cannot begin to tell you what and how I felt while the anointing was present. I hardly ever expressed what or how I felt. I was careful to give God all the glory because it all belonged to Him, and without the anointing, it would only be an empty performance. Being the choir director has inspired me and has contributed greatly to who I have become in shaping my ministry today.

As a senior in high school, I met my first love. I thought that my prince had come. He was tall and handsome. He had a voice that made you take notice and heart flutter. He was gifted and could sing, and he wanted to marry me. It made sense to me that my heart would fall for someone who shared a similar passion for music as I did. We discovered that we had some things in common such as a love for the church and music. Our connection through church and music seemed to propel us towards marriage. It was like "boy meets girl" and if you like each other, you get married. Well, that's exactly what happened. He bravely came to my dad and asked if he could marry me.

So right out of high school, I was married. I was the first out of all of my siblings to get married. After only a couple of months together, our marriage was over. It was over actually before it began. How could this happen? Why had

I not seen the signals? Did my family see any of this coming? I was so perplexed.

I worked the night shift, and when I came home one morning, he was gone. There were no warnings, no fights, or arguments. He left nothing behind. NOTHING! How well-planned could that have been? He just up and left his 18-year-old young bride alone. I was confused. I thought I did something wrong. I was so hurt, embarrassed, and so humiliated that I didn't want to face anyone outside of my family. It took me a long time to even want to talk about it. It took me some years. No one knew my hurt, my degree of pain, how I felt or what I was going through. God and my family were all I could depend on to console me. I was young and never really left home. I had a loving and caring family around me that helped me get through that nightmare.

As time went on, I discovered that he struggled with his sexuality. I didn't understand any of that, but I knew God must have had another plan for me. All of my hurt and pain could not be in vain. I always wondered if he would come back for us to try and start all over again. That was my hope.

As a young lady, I constantly envisioned myself being married and having my own family. I knew in my mind that's one of the things I wanted in life. It felt like the best was out there for me. Come on, I was a pastor's kid, a loved and respected young lady of integrity and dignity. Oh, well, that was some of my thoughts.

God did have another plan for me. As I continued on in life, I grew much stronger in my faith and in God. My dad was the pastor, and as one of his children, I was always involved in church work. I became more serious about doing ministry in the church with fewer distractions, meaning, I was now able to focus more on God and what he called me to do. As the years went on, through much prayer, I gained more and more strength in God. We never got divorced because of our religious beliefs. We remained separated.

Fast forwarding, twenty-four years later, my husband passed away, and I became a widow. I then resigned myself to the idea I might be a widow for the rest of my life. Amid those uncertainties, God was always by my side. My family was steadfast and helped me stay healthy in mind and spirit. I continued to have faith, to believe, to trust God, and to render service unto him. God opened doors for us to minister all over the world. I am grateful for every opportunity that He afforded me to minister.

Ten years later, I considered retiring to give more of myself to the work of the Lord in my local church and our community. I also wanted to be able to spend more time with my family and do some traveling.

As I was in the process of planning my retirement, God's plan for me started to unfold right before my eyes. He was working His plan out for my life, and I wasn't aware of all that was about to happen.

The Scripture says, "Trust in the Lord with all thine heart, and lean not to your own understanding," (Proverbs 3:5). I heard my dad quote this Scripture many times. This was another key moment that I was like, "Really God?" But I realize that I need to trust Him for my future as I have done in the past.

Here's how this stage of my new journey started. I was sitting at home one evening relaxing. I heard a ping on my phone. I received a simple text from a gentleman. I was like, "OMG should I respond or not?" Well, after contemplating on what to say to him, I responded the next day. I just wanted to take it a bit slowly in order to make the right decision. I was no longer 18 and I refused to go into another relationship blindly. After I responded, we began to share and get acquainted with each other. Within a couple of weeks, I then began to realize that God was at work with His plans for my life. I had no idea that this man would soon become my future husband and the love of my life. So, my Boaz, my Prince Charming, came many years later. God continues to be faithful to me in every way. He's a man that's highly respected, a minister of the gospel, and I must say, truly a God sent one. Trust me when I say I didn't know where this was going or where it would take me. All I knew in my spirit is that it was truly a God thing.

Again, the Scripture of trusting in God comes to mind. This was when I realized that God wasn't through with me. He was about to add another chapter to my life, which included marriage. Then, God set the wheels in motion to make things happen.

I finally got the opportunity to plan my dream wedding. I shopped with my sisters for the absolute best dress. I tried on so many gowns that I felt like Cinderella preparing for the ball of my life. I finally found the right dress. It was white with crystals all over the bodice down to the waist. It was absolutely gorgeous. I, like most brides, dieted to make sure the dress fit perfectly, and it did.

Speeding ahead to my wedding day, all of our family and friends showed up with love, support, and well wishes. The excitement was everywhere.

As I was in the bridal dressing room with my sister, my matron-of-honor, waiting for my cue, I heard the start of the ceremony, as the orchestra began to play. I could hardly stand the wait. The dancers and the singers were so amazing. I heard the buzz of people and the excitement of what was happening prior to my entrance.

As I entered the vestibule, my one and only brother, who was giving me away, stood there looking so handsome and proud, waiting at the entrance door to walk me up the aisles. I was so elated and excited. I practically danced all the way up the aisle to meet the love of my life. WOW!!! ....Finally!

We both said, "I do," and I can truly say that love has found me.

Amidst life's many disappointments, always remember to trust God in all of life's situations because He will always make a way that leads to your desired fulfillment.

Today I'm so thankful and grateful to God that He had an ultimate plan for my life, one in which I had to trust and believe His word.

if she gets sick? I wanted to trust God more and worry less as unexpected and unwelcome circumstances occurred, but the reality was that the harder I tried the more I worried. My instinctive response was to power through whatever it was to learn, understand, and do what was required of each challenge. And this would work initially but wasn't sustainable. I would exhaust my mind, body, and spirit as I continually worked harder and harder. Each transition and change seemed to bring with it increasing levels of stress and worry became a stowaway on my life journey.

Feelings of stress and anxiety are normal and universal. What we may not realize though, is that anxiety is often related to fear. We are well-aware of some of our fears and can name them, while others may be unconscious and deep in our thoughts. And not all fear is negative. Sometimes it's a healthy signal. The key is in identifying the source. Can I be honest and gracious with myself and admit what I'm afraid of so that I can address the core issue actively and productively? Could it be an invitation to growth, to deeper roots?

One day I was searching yet again for hair care products that would smooth my tight curls and tame the frizz and saw a product promising to do both. You mean I can get total control all at once? I'm in! After a few days of using it, I noticed something else I hadn't seen before. The words on the bottle seemed to shine in the morning light while everything else faded –

Tightly Wound

Who me? I had to chuckle as these words described my state of mind that morning worrying about this, anxious about that. I sensed a message from the bottle: Loosen control and your worry will lessen.

Of course, the natural response is to attempt to control the situation. We think that mastering the circumstance will eliminate our fear and anxiety, but what if it's still messy after our best attempts? I couldn't even make my babies fall asleep when I wanted them to. What if I'm a bad parent? I will be forever grateful to the trusted and wise people in my life with whom I could share these feelings and thoughts. With their help, I began to understand that my beliefs (spoken or unspoken) led to my thoughts, which guided my actions. With their help, I learned that I could intentionally pursue a way of life that consciously diminished worry. Here are three approaches that help calm my anxious thoughts and replace them with peace.

Silence and Solitude

In a world where fast-paced, fully scheduled lifestyles are more the norm than the exception, it can be a serious challenge just to hear ourselves think. Even if you have to schedule it, it's important to check in regularly with yourself. I started by setting up a chair in the basement where during the early morning hours, I could pray, worship, read the Bible, and journal. Sometimes I would sing along with worship music or play it quietly in the background to set the atmosphere. I also love lighting a candle. My favorite fragrance is a blend of frankincense and myrrh. I wasn't always as focused as I would have liked in these moments and sometimes, I'd even doze off, but eventually, I learned to make a habit of sitting quietly in the presence of the Lord. The goal is to quiet our souls and pay attention to the beliefs and thoughts that are inside of us.

In addition to daily solitude, I plan monthly or quarterly check-in times. This doesn't have to be elaborate. It could be as simple as spending extended time in my bedroom on a Saturday or Sunday morning. It could be a walk along a nature trail. These opportunities look different during various seasons in my life. What does this look like for you?

Gratitude

When we begin to recognize and acknowledge what we're truly thinking and feeling, the reality is that it's not always pleasant. We may find disappointment, frustration, and more rising to the surface depending on the current state of our lives and those around us. It could lead to a downward spiral if we aren't careful. My intent is not to deny the circumstances but to choose the lens through which I will view them. There is well-documented research on the relationship between gratitude and self-reported well-being across the life span. If you are looking for an evidence-based strategy to bring a measure of peace into your life, you might consider starting a daily gratitude list.

Over a decade ago, I began listing what I was grateful for throughout the day. The process directs my attention to a range of people, places, things, and opportunities for which I'm thankful. I wrote about the sound of rain on my roof, the smile and wave of a toddler walking in the neighborhood, delicious dinner prepared by my husband, awakening to bright sunshine in the summer... you get the idea. How would keeping a record of daily thanks make a difference in your well-being?

Thought Choices

Paying attention to my thoughts has been the most challenging aspect of my growth. I have taken steps forward only to slip back into automatic thoughts that are based in worry and fear. Usually, this happens when I'm trying to deal with it all by myself. The hopeful news is that I can identify the thoughts more readily now and replace the ones that are not based on truth. What's key is that I have learned not only to hear my thoughts but to take it a step further and share them with God. In the loving presence of the Lord, I find clarity and peace. In the Scriptures, I find new ways of thinking and processing that I'm able to model along the pathway to peace. They give me a framework through which to process my issues, concerns, and thoughts. They reveal underlying beliefs that fuel unwanted thoughts. "Whenever my busy thoughts were out of control, the soothing comfort of your presence calmed me down and overwhelmed me with delight."

What thoughts have you played over and over in your mind that you want to be rid of? Tell the Lord about them.

Ridding ourselves of toxic thoughts is not a self-help project. We need Jesus to help us get to the "...authentic and real, honorable and admirable, beautiful and respectful, pure and holy, merciful and kind..." ways of thinking and being. We are changed as we spend time in the presence of our Holy and Loving God, and He leads us to a peace that is not moved by circumstances.

CHAPTER FOUR

YOU ARE STRONG

THELMA HAYES

PRELUDE

Quitting was never an option for me as a child.

Mom would stare me in the face and say, "You are strong, God will make a way."

Then at school, we were always being told, "Don't give up."

I recall learning the poem "Don't Quit" by John Greenleaf Whittier in elementary school during a time when social injustices ruled the communities. Having attended a segregated school from kindergarten until seventh grade, our teachers impressed upon us the spirit of never quitting or giving up. My homelife echoed the same message, but at home, the message was grounded in the Bible and in our daily experiences of overcoming poverty, needs, and lack. My mother's message to each of her children was, "Be strong because you are strong." The story, *You Are Strong*, reflects on childhood experiences of both my mother and me. I pray you are blessed and inspired as you engage these stories.

"It's when things seem worst that you must not quit."

~ John Greenleaf Whittier

...

On a cold and stormy winter night around 6:30, the labor pains began. The fire in the stove of the small southern wooden home was burning cozily as the labor grew more and more intense. Who would have thought that this child would decide to arrive earlier than expected? Not her mother nor her grandmother who had been brought over to the house by her father to help his wife who was beginning to struggle in labor. The storm, though expected, had grown more severe than the forecast and the wood-burning stove worked hard to keep the home warm. Three other small children were already tucked into their beds under their warm heavy handmade blankets. Blankets that were made from bits of old clothing and coats that all had outgrown and had been cut into small patches and then carefully sewn together by their mother and grandmother. Though not asleep yet, they knew not to get out of bed for fear of discipline.

As the labor grew more intense, so did the weather, as if it were in deep competition with the labor pains! Thus, the possibility of getting out to the hospital lessened with the increasing contractions and intensified storm. This baby was going to have to be delivered at home! An African American woman in labor in the South did not warrant an emergency ambulance in this small town in North Carolina, where Jim Crow laws were in full effect. As the labor continued, the grandmother did her best to help her daughter become as comfortable as possible until the midwife arrived. The harsh windy rains blowing fiercely outside had caused the delay of the midwife who had to walk three miles to get to the home and assist.

Upon arrival, the midwife stepped in to do what she had done so many times in her community, preparing to deliver the baby and support the mother through the process. But it became apparent that something was not right. The mom was bleeding more than usual and becoming weaker and weaker by the moment.

"PRAY, pray, pray!" she shouted to the dad and grandmother. If this child and mom are to survive tonight, we best be praying and praying hard! Come on gal."

The soft words of the midwife coached the mom in labor.

"You can do this. You know the Lawd is here with you and you gone have this baby and ya'll gone be fine," she chanted.

The dad put more wood and coal into the stove so that the house would be warm when the baby arrived. The grandmother sang her prayers to the Lord and sat expectantly watching the midwife do what she had done for three births in this house before. What seemed like an eternity passed until suddenly there was the sound of a faint cry.

"It's a girl", the midwife announced. "Mom is alright, too. God done blessed this house wit a girl."

That night was March 9th in a small southern town in North Carolina, I was born early during one of the worst storms of the year. My mother tells me that although I was tiny, I was strong.

From the time I can remember, I recall my mother always told me these words, "You are strong."

There have been times when I have embraced those words. There have been times when I felt those words were said just to get me to shut up or not complain. There have been times when I have believed those words and rejected them too. "You are STRONG"!" The words have impacted the way that I lived my life. I have so many stories to tell that depict the essence of the word "strong". My birth story, however, is perhaps the greatest of those stories. Why, because of my mother's strength and perseverance, I was born into this world. My strength or ability to be strong is a direct gift of love from my mother.

From Where, My Strength Comes

Now allow me to share more about this wonderful woman that I call mother. She was born in the 1930's to parents who were sharecroppers. Her father was the product of a racially mixed relationship during the early 1900's when mixed marriage was illegal in the state of North Carolina. His father was Caucasian and never married his mother, although they had seven children together.

Mom had a rugged beginning at birth. She was born with a dark complexion which angered her mulatto father. He had married a lighter complexioned African American and wished for brighter skinned children. My mother was the second oldest child and the oldest girls of four children born to her parents. Her younger sister and brother had a much fairer complexion than she. As the oldest girl, she bore much responsibility to help take care of the younger children and the home. Her childhood was robbed away because of the burdensome responsibilities of bringing water from the well, carrying wood for the fire, and cleaning out the stalls for the animals. Her younger sister was not required to do much because of her favored position in the family.

Mom loved school and learning and was very smart at it too. But the harsh realities of sharecroppers' lives often interrupted her pursuit of education. Not only were her parent's sharecroppers, but they had also little to no formal education and were often cheated out of their earnings, leaving them dependent on the landowner for loans to make it through winter months. My grandfather resorted to making homemade liquor in a still carefully hidden in the cornfields. The sales brought income but also misery to my mom and her siblings. My grandfather would often become drunk and lash out in anger towards his children. His anger and outburst resulted in my grandmother fleeing and leaving her children with their dad until she could find adequate work. Mom took over the role of caring for the house and lost her privilege to attend school consistently. But she never stopped learning. The Bible and a few books in the house became her source of comfort as she would steal away with the lantern and read after going to bed. Strength began building up inside of her. She developed a strength that would cause her to rely on the Word of God as her source of truth and escape from the cruel surroundings she found herself in.

Finding her strength through trusting God spurred my mother to be the strong woman she is today. Although her life was filled with many challenges, she trusted that God would always see her through. She was determined to transfer the essential truths to her children. Every day, she reminded us that we were strong and that our strength comes for the Lord.

STRENGTH FOR THE MOMENT
THELMA HAYES

You only need strength for the moment,
Not for the future nor the past.
You only need strength for the moment,
For the trial you are facing won't last.
You only need strength for the moment,
For there is a power that will see you through.
You only need strength for the moment
Stand still; see what God will do!

Strength doesn't always look like victory,
Sometimes it's full of pain.
Strength doesn't always look like triumph,

There are times when there's no gain.
Strength doesn't look like peace,
For the storm is often roaring,
But strength comes from the Father,
Whose promises are always pouring.

God's promises are always pouring out to you,
His beloved and blood-washed child.
God's promises are always surrounding you,
Although you may not wear a smile.
God's promises are always sustaining,
Dependable and always kept.
He promises to wipe away all tears,
Of his faithful children who have wept.

You are strong says the Father,
The Son and the Holy Ghost.
As long as you trust and remember,
That we love you the most.

REFLECTION AND CONNECTION

As you read these few pages, what personal experience did you connect to that demonstrated that you have a strength beyond yourself? How do you reconnect with those moments to push you forward when new trials come your way?

PRAYER

Heavenly Father, you have called me to be your child and I trust in you. Your name is great and greatly to be praised. When I am weak, Father, you are my strength. Your strength moves miraculously into and through my circumstances to remind me that you are dependable. I trust that you will never leave me. I choose to rest in your strength and become as you said, "Run and not be weary." Read Isaiah 40:30 – 31.

CHAPTER FIVE

MY LEGACY LETTER... GOLDEN NUGGETS OF INSPIRATION FOR CHALLENGES TO COME

LINDA WILLIAMS

PRELUDE

Dear Family and Friends,

Come travel along with me on an adventuresome excursion, which includes a few brief journeys of experiences along my life's colorful pathway. This life-long voyage has provided me several amazing narratives, and as I recollect the many impactful encounters that brought me to where I am today, I am both fascinated and astounded. Fascinated by the range of scenarios and astounded by the way they worked together to shape who I am today. Many of you may have shared or will share similar trials and triumphs throughout the years, from childhood through early adulthood to marriage and present day. Relive a few of those with me and reap some **Golden Nuggets of Inspiration.**

...

Journey #1: Amazing Childhood

"That was good, now say it for me one more time, a little louder."

These are the words I heard from my awesome Mom, Rena B. Hammond, who was teaching me the sixty-six books of the Bible when I was almost four years old. Now for the setting. As a challenge to the youth in Sunday School, prizes would be given to any child who could recite all sixty-six books of the Bible in order. So, of course, my Mom, who was a high school teacher, educator by profession, and a Sunday school teacher, brought the challenge home to my brother and me. Since he was four years older, he could read, but I was just beginning to read, so I required some motherly assistance. Within a few days, we both were ready, and during the special program at church, we both recited them perfectly, with several other boys and girls as well. At the time, I didn't realize that I was the youngest one on stage, a recurring phenomenon that I didn't know at the time, would pervade throughout my youth. A gold bracelet with the Ten Commandments was the excellent prize received, which I deeply cherished, wore to school when I finally started kindergarten, and still have in my jewelry chest!

So many people in the audience were amazed, which I learned later that a child so young could have memorized and delivered so confidently the books of the Bible, in front of a church full of people with no hesitation. This would be one of the first of many such opportunities to participate at an early age in speaking events at church, school, and in the community, despite the naysayers that thought, "She is too young."

Later on, after I learned to read, another element came into play. I was literally able to memorize words on a page, just as they were written, whether typed, printed, or hand-written...pages at a time. So, if you wrote me a seven-page poem, the entire passage would be memorized page by page and could be recited, as if I was literally seeing the words on the page after the fact. Needless to say, this *gift* was very helpful in all levels of schooling from elementary through college, and even later into professional licenses and certifications.

Ironically, I just took a photographic memory challenge on my iPhone, and to my surprise, it said I was in the 1% of folks with that gift.

ENCOURAGEMENT NUGGET

...when there are discouragers who may be saying things like you're too young or you're too...anything, just keep your higher focus and continue to go above and beyond all expectations. Don't allow others' negativity, doubts, and insecurities to limit your achievements. "A man's gift makes room for him, and brings him before great men," (Proverbs 18:16).

Journey #2: The School Years

Having grown up in a small town of only about 10,000 people, many of my classmates remained the same from elementary through high school. It was truly awesome to have experienced and enjoyed our 40th year high school reunion—Rancocas Valley Regional High School (RVRHS) a couple of years ago!

In retrospect of our local school system, I can honestly say that the current issues of race, etc., were not evident nor experienced at any level of my education, from my perspective. Fortunately, I was able to excel in academics, usually at the top of my classes, and not receiving my first "B" until I was in 7th or 8th grade. Thankfully throughout high school, my GPA remained between 5.0 and 5.5, as we were on a 5-point grading scale, with 5.5 being an "A+". Graduating as #5 in my class of 300 was truly an honor, as well as being president of the National Junior Honor Society (NJHS).

Having a mom who was a high school educator and a dad, Ozie Sr., who was a 25-year veteran chief warrant officer in the army, established a standard of excellence in our home. And of course, having a big brother, Ozie, who was four years older and a very close cousin, Rosalyn, who was ten years older and lived with us during the summers, always kept that sense of comradery and competition alive. Personally, I always had a goal of putting forth my best effort in whatever I did, including getting the best grades I could in school, doing my best in games or any competition, for example board games, which we would play into the wee hours of the morning during the holidays, card games, 8-ball in billiards, which our dad taught us when I was in 8th grade and we got our first pool table, playing "PIG" in the backyard basketball hoop, acting in a church play, reciting MLK's I Have a Dream speech for black history programs, selling girl scout cookies door-to-door, playing hop-scotch, or whatever.

"You are never too old to set another goal or to

dream a new dream."

~ C. S. Lewis

Communities were so much closer when I look back. As kids, our neighbors looked out for each other, and we could be chastised by a neighbor, who would then inform our parents. What ensued after that varied by family, but in general, it wasn't pretty. Neighbors would take walks through the community, come sit on your porch, and catch up on what was new and exciting. Those were, indeed, the good ole days.

As noted earlier, the social climate did not deter my participation nor inclusion in sports, basketball and softball, band (1st chair clarinetist), NJHS and NHS, nor Red Oak yearbook as editor.

By far, one of the most exciting high school experiences was my path to college. After doing very well with the PSAT's in my sophomore year, several colleges invited me to apply and offered scholarships. I remember getting so much mail from schools across the country and thinking, "Which one is right for me?" My counselor, Dr. Hess, always encouraged me, told me about some of the pros and cons of different schools, and was definitely a positive influence during my high school years. I remember getting the letter and finding out I was accepted at the school of my choice, Michigan State, during my junior year, which was unbelievable! And they offered me a scholarship. Senior year was such a great time of really enjoying school and of preparation and great experiences; all with no pressure concerning college acceptance. One exciting event that I'll always remember was the band trip we took my senior year, to a series of southern colleges to perform, participate in parades, and experience a touch of college life before actually attending. Since I had been voted band secretary, I got to help organize the band trip under the direction of our band leader, Mr. Amos. The extensive work in coordination of this trip, from transportation to meal stops to talking to the college liaisons really laid the groundwork of coordination of many trips and events for business organizations, churches, and family groups, that would come later in life.

Looking back, my school years were tremendous and laid some lasting foundational tenets that permeate my business, personal, and social pathways to this day. I can truthfully say that I never liked to miss one day of school!

And remember the photographic memory element from Journey #1? Well, it certainly kicked in, particularly in high school and college.

I remember my last Final Exam in college, the professor had given us five potential questions, two of which would be on the Blue Book essay exam. Needless to say, I wrote out all five multi-page responses, and when it came time for the test, I wrote word-for-word what I had previously laid out. It was as if I saw the 8.5 x 11 sheet of notebook paper, as I was writing, in the Blue Book. Thankfully, I was one of the first to finish, and received a 4.0!

"In order to succeed, we must first believe that we can."

~ Nikos Kazantazkis

Some naysayers told me that I should only apply to in-state colleges, that I would never get accepted to a big school because the competition would be too steep and that I would not be able to keep up or excel.

ENCOURAGEMENT NUGGET

The world is full of naysayers, all of them eager to shout you down at the slightest indication that you might transcend mediocrity. Our job isn't to join that group, but to silence it by accomplishing things so great and unimaginable that they are too awed to speak. - Jon Morrow

Tune out the naysayers, tune into your own courage, and take a bold step toward the passion-filled life you really want.

~ Oprah Winfrey

"For with God nothing shall be impossible."

~ Luke 1:37

Journey #3: The Early Married Years

"You will NEVER have a baby!"

Can you imagine being told that after waiting for years to get started on the family phase of your relationship and hearing that from not just *your* doctor, but two other highly recommended doctors as well? After the initial shock, sadness, questioning, and all that goes with it, my faith kicked in, and I immediately concluded: I'm talking to the WRONG doctors! I know that He knows the desires of my heart to be a mom, and the desires of my husband's heart to be a dad. I need a doctor that will be in faith with me, take me through what needs to happen, and get us to where we need to be to welcome a baby into our family.

"Believe you can and you're halfway there."

~ Theodore Roosevelt

So, the search began. Within a few days, I was actually having a conversation with LaRue Ford, who was married to our renowned musician friend, Steven Ford.

After explaining the situation and what I had been through, she immediately said, "You should go see my doctor, she's wonderful."

So of course, I thought nothing of taking the hour trip to her doctor's office in Philadelphia. After the examination, Dr. Isa Velez told us that she had a plan that could optimally result in the ability to get pregnant after about six months of treatment. Caveat: I would need to do daily self-injections that would get me ready for a surgical procedure that would in turn, open the door of possibility to conceive. Without hesitation, we agreed that this would be the path. Did I forget to mention that needles of any sort are not my favorite, as it normally takes at least three tries before a nurse can draw blood, but I also believe that all things are possible through Christ.

Fast forward six months, the injection regimen was followed to the letter, and the surgery, my first ever, was successful! Now the window of opportunity was open. With the surgery being done in November, we were told that we only had until February, three months, to conceive. No pressure, right? Our daughter's birthday is in November, so you do the math. Yes, February was the month!

For ten fantastic years, our early married life was awesome, full of fun, travel, spur of the moment excursions, and getting to know each other. We proposed that we would schedule an annual vacation, so it was not left to chance, which typically turned out to be an international cruise. Although this model may not be for everyone, it definitely worked for us and allowed us the independence to enjoy and experience married life, each other, and unified service to our church and community, *before* having children, which we planned.

Music played a significant role in our relationship and service. Having taught myself to play piano at an early age on an old player piano, then moving on to a surprise Christmas present from my parents of a spinet piano, I enjoyed playing hymns and anthems and contemporary gospel. With the ability to read music, from my many years of playing clarinet in school, my main motivation and goal for learning to play the piano was to be able to play in church, which soon came to fruition. The pastor's wife, Mrs. Bobbitt, after hearing me play, immediately plugged me in to playing for Sunday school, vacation Bible school, then Sunday morning and evening service, accompanying the senior choir, and finally leading and playing for the youth ensemble. Along the way, I also learned to play the Hammond B-3 organ, which was an added bonus.

Included in this musical journey was the musical infusion during college and our early marriage. In college, I met my husband, Winston, in the backdrop of Michigan State University's Black Orpheus Choir. In preparing for our spring concert, we were at a dress rehearsal at the concert venue. Winston was one of the choir accompanists. He was on the organ stool when our director, Jackie Davis, gave us a short break. Most choir members and musicians left the auditorium, but I chose to stay. Totally out of character, I went over to the organ stool and initiated a conversation, something I had *never* done before. It had always been the other way around, with the gentleman coming up to me. We talked and talked, immediately clicked, and the rest is history. Being a part of Orpheus also allowed us to get some early peeks into artists during their infancy, who would become gospel greats, i.e. The Testimonials performed as Orpheus' special guests, who later went on to become the renowned group known as The Winans. We also heard the Winans Part 2, which featured then unknown BeBe and CeCe Winans.

After leaving college and getting married, I became involved in the music of our local church in Philadelphia, directing the choir and singing on the praise team. A little later, I became involved as a director of the Mass Choir, which combined multiple churches of our organization city-wide, totaling approximately 50-75 choir members, and traveled throughout the region and beyond, doing ministry. Involvement in these musical organizations continued after we were married and during my pregnancy.

Phenomenal is the only word to describe my pregnancy, *never* experiencing morning sickness, barely showing for the first six months, fully mobile, and totally active including attending Mass Choir rehearsal in Philadelphia on the Monday before delivery on Wednesday.

"I believe it's time," were my words to Winston as I experienced my first contraction late Tuesday evening.

We called the doctor, and she said she'd meet us at HUP (Hospital of the University Pennsylvania). After arriving, only one more contraction was experienced before the meds were administered in preparation for the C-Section. Within two hours of arrival at the hospital, our beautiful baby girl, Brittanye Patryce Williams, was brought into the world...healthy and vibrant...the answer to many prayers. And Brittanye continues to be an extraordinary blessing in our lives and others!

ENCOURAGEMENT NUGGET

When you receive multiple "No's," just bear in mind, you may be talking to the wrong person(s) (or doctor(s) in my case).

"If opportunity doesn't knock, build a door."

~ Milton Berle

"For I know the plans I have for you," declares the LORD, "plans to prosper you and not to harm you, plans to give you hope and a future."

~ Jeremiah 29:11

Journey #4: An Open Hand

"If I can help somebody as I pass along, If I can cheer somebody with a word or a song, If I can show somebody he is traveling wrong, then my living shall not be in vain."

~ Alma Bazel Androzzo

You may have heard these lyrics from a popular hymn, which also happened to be my Mom's favorite song. And I would have to say, "Then My Living Shall Not Be in Vain," was definitely a part of her legacy, which she demonstrated daily and passed on to me and my brother.

My First Job

When I was in early high school, having a brother, Ozie, who worked at the local children's home, gave me a deeper insight and perspective into young people who did not have the same opportunities, growing up, which were afforded to me. With a focus on helping children and their families become productive members of society, the children's home provided residential treatment services, including special education, counseling, family therapy, and recreation. Already having his B.A. in Social Work, I remember Ozie coming home from work on a Saturday looking through our closets to find clothes for some of the residents because he wanted to bring them to church on Sunday and they didn't have clothes to wear. After finding some outfits and bringing them to church, all of us would literally walk directly across the street to our house after church to eat dinner together. Having guests for dinner on Sundays or throughout the week was a regular occurrence, for two reasons: 1) my mom was a home economics major and an excellent cook and 2) everyone knew our door was always open, especially when there were special afternoon services which were almost every week.

So, during my summers home from college, my brother opened the door to my getting hired by the children's home auxiliary facility, known as the youth shelter. As opposed to the children's home which offered more long-term accommodations for the residents. The youth shelter offered more temporary facilities for middle-school to high school-aged children, who were either waiting to be placed in a family's home or being transferred to another facility. Another caveat with this position was that I was only a few years older than many of the residents. However, I had nothing to fear because my big brother was well-known and respected by both staff and residents.

Although I didn't realize it at the time, I found myself always wanting to give extra help. I would bring some of the girls my cleaned clothes from home, especially if they were scheduled to go home, on a special trip, or to another residence. When I had the late-night shift, I also found myself staying up late with some of them, just hearing their stories and offering some encouragement about school and/or their families. I remember in particular one girl who was actually contemplating hurting herself because she didn't feel she had anything to live for. The talk that night seemed so natural, just reassuring her that there were people who loved her and cared about her, and that she had so much to look forward to, as her life was really just beginning. We talked for hours, and when the morning supervisor came in, I filled her in on what had happened, and I remember her being so impressed, because this girl opened up to no one. The good news is that within two weeks she went back to her family, and the last report we received she was doing well.

Of course, I didn't know it at the time, but that session would be the prelude for future help sessions, which would continue for years to come, and are on-going even now, with family, friends, co-workers, and strangers.

Looking back, I can see that pouring into others has truly been passed down and has been a core component of my family from my mom's generous open heart, always willing to help, to my Dad working at the NJ State Home for Boys and pouring into them, to my brother, who now has his doctorate in social work, and runs groups to help those in need. From this legacy, I now see why I enjoy mentoring at all levels, including youth, having been involved in church tutoring ministries; mentoring co-workers, including starting a volunteer after-work class to help three of my task leaders to get their PMP (Project Management Professional) certifications, which they successfully achieved; and mentoring family members on multiple levels, including personal, business, and individual project strategies.

As family members and friends moved from the mid-west and other places to the east coast, we were fortunate to have the opportunity to again pour into others by providing a home where they could get grounded while they were trying to establish themselves. Over the years, we thankfully have been able to host and help at least 12 family members on their journeys.

Have you ever experienced being in line at a store check-out, a fast-food establishment, or a restaurant, and you found out after reaching for your wallet that someone had taken care of your bill? Regularly, I would go to a restaurant at the Federal Triangle in D.C., for breakfast, and whoever happened to be behind me in line would get blessed in this way. It got to the point where those at the registers knew me and would just give that nod that confirmed the next person was about to experience something nice.

Typically, the response would be one of surprise, with many expressing that, "No one has ever done that for me before," or "I'm going to do that for someone else."

The best analogy regarding my motivation for mentoring and helping others is that of an *open hand*. I believe that giftings, knowledge, experience, and assets were endowed upon me for a reason. So, I have two choices: 1) to keep everything I have inside and use as a personal growth mechanism or 2) to open my hand and help others with the blessings that were bestowed on me. My belief is that the *open hand* is my mantra to help and bless others as I have been blessed. The knowledge, experience, and wisdom that has been imparted to me shall likewise be imparted to others.

"My mission in life is not merely to survive, but to thrive; and to do so with some passion, some compassion, some humor, and some style."

~ Maya Angelou

ENCOURAGEMENT NUGGET

Know that you are blessed to be a blessing to others. Acknowledge that the wisdom, experience, knowledge, and assets you have are not meant to stay within you in your closed hand, but to be extended to others with your *open hand*. Be encouraged to step outside that comfort zone and pay it forward.

Then, you too can say, "Then my living shall not be in vain."

"Give, and it shall be given unto you; good measure, pressed down, and shaken together, and running over, shall men give into your lap. For with the same measure that you measure it shall be measured to you again."

~ Luke 6:38

CHAPTER SIX

WHAT WAS... IS NOT WHAT IS!

ORDEAN SIMMONS

PRELUDE

How did she get here, the intellect who was on the school debate team, the AP student, athlete, and member of her church choir? How did she let her life get to this point where she would be standing in this wound so deep? Would she learn how to turn her wound into wisdom, or would she give it the power to devour her every being? Would she run towards destruction or walk in the direction of love? What she will find is with the God of a second chance, it is never about your circumstance.

...

She looks over at the heart monitor next to her hospital bed. The red and green lines jump rhythmically across the screen keeping time with her baby's heartbeat. The echoes of his movement can be heard from the monitor and fills up the small hospital room, leaving her to only imagine what he will look like. She touches her belly to feel his arms and legs press against the palms of her hands as he stretches in search of room in his temporary home.

He is here now. Here in the world that he has yet to meet. As beautiful as new life is and in a moment that most would yearn for, she can't help but feel sad and alone. Pregnancy at 17 felt like death to a young girl who had a promising future; a future that now had faded. She never imagined this would be her story. Her dreams as a child weren't any different from most little girls who envisioned they would grow up to have that big house with a nice yard, a husband, and three kids, or maybe five kids like Claire Huxtable, a lawyer. She hoped one day to become a criminal defense attorney or prosecutor who would eventually become a judge and pillar of her community. Both studious and quick on her feet, she had the brains and tenacity to achieve it. That dream now seemed like the fantasy of a girl she used to know. She was unrecognizable to herself and her parents. She had a mother and father who doted on her every chance that they had. They were once so proud of the girl who was respectful, kind, and loving. The daughter that teachers, friends, and family saw to be the ideal child who some had hoped they could one day have. Little did they know, she was not what they should be hoping for. At least that's what she felt. She let down the little sister that used to look up to her. Her life had taken a turn down a road that left her trying to find and catch up to the person she used to be.

Her younger sister and best friends had just dropped by to see how she was doing before they headed out to celebrate a birthday weekend. It was Saturday, September 21st. The three of them stood at the foot of her bed and engaged in casual lighthearted conversation. As casual as it can get when you feel like you no longer can relate to the people who you grew up with. They all looked happy and she tried to do the same, attempting to make herself believe nothing had changed or at least if it did, then eventually it would all go back to normal. She wanted to be able to hang out and do all the things that a 17-year-old should be doing on a Saturday. But the hard reality was it couldn't go back to the way things had been. She was on bed rest in a hospital with doctors and nurses who saw her only as a statistic. A statistic that brought shame to her family and wasn't worth the effort to try and save. The only thing that gave her any reassurance was knowing she had her family in her corner. As much as she had hurt them, they never gave up on her. It wasn't easy by any means as it took many months of praying, crying, and sleepless nights before they could realize the new reality that they would endure.

The night before checking into the hospital felt like a lonely scary hole. That Friday led to a visit with the family physician she had known since early childhood. Having him check that the baby was okay was all she needed so that she could go home and start the next day over.

What Was

To understand this moment in the hospital requires a bit of the back story. The administrators at her school moved her into a program earlier that month that had been designed for somewhat wayward or troubled teens. It was a program for high school students to learn while working in the community with various businesses and organizations. Up until that point, she never needed or had been considered for alternative education; however, the school saw it to be beneficial for "someone in her situation". Grades had dropped, and her attendance was poor. Guidance counselors hadn't done much guiding and suggested she give up on the idea of becoming a lawyer. Looking back, she thinks they may have seen that program to be more beneficial for them, keeping the image of the pregnant teen off of school grounds.

That same day she missed the bus from school that would take her to the business work program; so, she walked for nearly an hour in the hot sun trying to get there. Cramps in her stomach and back had her stopping every few minutes to get some rest and second-guessing if she should or even could make the trip, but tired of giving up she kept moving. The day proved itself to be one that she wishes she could take back. The cramps continued to get worse as she was instructed to lift and pull heavy materials to build something that now she can't remember what it was for. This was a project that they had been working on in the days previously. Not knowing or understanding the potential harm she may have been causing to her baby, she continued to push through. When the pain became unbearable and she started spotting, she quietly left and got on a city bus downtown to see her family doctor who was the only person she felt she could trust with her concern. Meeting with Dr. Maharaj that day was a trying experience as she considered him to be a part of her family. He was one of those doctors who genuinely cared. You could hear the care in his voice and see it in his eyes whenever he spoke to you. He would give you that parent glare when you weren't listening or give you the warmest smile when you shared little wins.

She hadn't seen Dr. Maharaj in months if not close to a year; he was unpleasantly surprised to see the little baby bump that preceded her when she walked in the room. She had not been getting prenatal checkups out of pure ignorance and partly shame and so in the five months of being pregnant this was only her second visit to a doctor. The first was to get an ultrasound and determine the sex of the baby; the second was at that moment to ensure everything was okay. The visit was short as Dr. Maharaj upon a quick examination, confirmed he could see the baby's head and she was in jeopardy of losing him at any time. He advised her to get to the hospital as soon as possible. Fear and anger started to settle in, but she tried not to show it. She had to be a big girl because she had gotten herself into big girl problems. All she knew to do at that time was pray.

By this time, it was rush hour and she got onto a crowded bus to go to the hospital closest to home. That bus ride was long and emotional as she struggled to fight back the tears and squash the lump in her throat. She hoped someone would offer up their seat to a pregnant woman on the verge of losing her baby. Of course, they didn't know it; but maybe they would see the pain in her face and sense what she was going through.

Walking up to the emergency room triage desk while gently cupping her belly, she managed to tell the nurse on duty why she was there. She tried her best to not let anyone make her feel ashamed. Hoping that they would give her priority, she took her seat alone in the back of the waiting room silently crying for her baby. Although it was not an ideal situation to be in, she wanted this baby. It couldn't be denied. She had fallen in love with the life that had begun to grow inside her. She talked to him every night and listened to the heartbeat with her stethoscope that was a gift meant to encourage her future possibilities. She became infatuated with becoming the best mother she thought she could be and imagined this new life would be someone she could give all her love to and he would love her back just as much. She would be responsible for someone who would depend on her and that gave her the illusion of achievement.

The slow nightmare that seemed to begin that day started to ring some truth in her mind. Everything else in her life she had always been able to envision in its entirety and see it come to fruition, but she was never able to see past her pregnancy. She couldn't see giving birth to this baby or taking him home and raising him. That vision always seemed to cut short. Although blurry, it almost was giving her a clear message.

The Waiting Room

By now, it's dusk and the small number of patients who were waiting to be seen had come and gone. Her 3rd-grade teacher and elementary school principal walked into the waiting room of the hospital. Ms. Mason was one of those teachers you remembered for life. Not only was she trendy with her always well-manicured nails, double ear piercings, and perfectly styled hair, but she was also extremely caring. She saw something in that little girl that most would dismiss. A flood of memories came back in a flash as both teachers walked over and sat across from her. There was the time in 3rd grade that she advocated for an advance to 7th grade English as she saw the reading and writing capabilities of a student that wasn't being nurtured. Not giving up on making sure those talents were seen, she had the school library publish the short story written by that little girl who she was proud to call her student. That same little girl she took under her wing in 6th grade and campaigned that a secondary leading role be created for after her audition turned her down for the lead role of Snow White in the school musical. Although she was humbly aware, and evidence from the faculties' reactions during the auditions showed that she carried the part of the character a little better than her fellow student, logically Snow White was just that, white. Anything was possible and nothing would stop her from going for what she rightfully wanted to obtain. Snapped back into the reality of the moment by their approach, the memories faded.

She could see the worry in Ms. Masons' face as she approached the 5'4 girl not weighing more than 130 lbs. sitting in her overalls alone at night in the ER with bloodshot eyes from crying. That moment was a pause and brought an onslaught of more memories. It took her back and reminded her of the childhood aspirations she once had and now she found herself trying to avert eye contact with this woman. The question she hoped wouldn't be was asked, "Are you okay?" That was enough. There's something about those three words that can send the strongest person to their demise. She remembers Ms. Mason stepping across the aisle to sit next to and comfort her as she shared the news. There wasn't much said after that she can remember, but she does remember the look on her teacher's face. That same look of feeling disheartened and disappointed that she had become so accustomed to seeing from the people who she thought cared. Observing that she was alone in the ER, they both encouraged her to use the payphone nearby to call home and let her family know what happened and where she was.

The next day, Saturday, she was diagnosed with having an incompetent cervix, a condition she learned would need to be addressed early with any future pregnancies. This would require a cerclage to be performed to avoid a miscarriage or preterm birth around the second trimester. They recommended her to a prestigious hospital downtown and arranged for her to be transferred to the Catholic care facility on that Monday for them to place the cervical stitch and monitor the health of the baby. This was good news to her. In 2 more days, her baby would be saved. She could finish up school and start preparations for her soon to be bundle of love, but God saw it differently.

Then, Sunday in the hospital started out quiet. After church, her father came and spent some time with her in the room and they watched the tiny, mounted television together in silence. Knowing how her father felt and considering how he was handling it; she saw this as a nice gesture as simple as it was. He had taken it the hardest when he initially got the news. Acting out of anger he reacted by having her leave the house but with intervention, counseling, and much prayer from their home church pastor, he was able to address the pain she had caused him in a way that showed he still cared.

As the evening went on, the pains of childbirth began to rear its head. The contractions that had been little distractions and were few and far in between, had suddenly become intensely excruciating. The monitor she had been strapped to the entire weekend that kept a record of those contractions, alerted her nurse that they were getting worse. The tiny room became filled with hospital staff and out of sheer discomfort, her father excused himself as he sensed what was about to transpire. It was time. She was in labor. His baby girl was having a baby.

Wheeling her bed out of the room and down the hall to the labor and delivery room was like a slow-motion hallucination. The lights in the hallway seemed to be brighter than normal. This couldn't be happening. We only had to wait one more day to see the doctors that could "fix this". She wasn't ready and she definitely knew the baby wasn't ready. This didn't seem fair. Why was this happening? What she feared was happening and she couldn't help but let the tears run down her face. She knew what all of this meant. It just so happened that the father of the baby, his closest friend, and her mother at that very same time were making their way down the hall for a visit. She recalls the look of panic that came across her mother's face and the look of terror the father tried to mask as they realized what was happening.

From what she could remember, the delivery room was cold and bare. There was nothing around to welcome a new life into the world. As they prepped her to deliver, everything began to become a blur. It was a quick delivery from what she remembered. She heard no joyful sound of a baby crying that all parents welcome just complete silence. Weighing a little under 1 pound and being the length of a size 9 shoe, baby Edwards was wrapped in a blanket and held by the grandmother and father he would never get to know. In that cold bare room, she was left to find her new purpose as she got to hold her son for the first and last time.

What Is

It didn't matter that I no longer had to bear the weight of being a teen mother. I held the hurt that I birthed for a long time. Everything after that moment did not matter. This wasn't a moment of relief for me. Many may think it's done and over with and time to move on, but it was quite the opposite. The hurt and anger I felt was severe and all I could do was question God. Why didn't he save my baby? Why would he let me go through this pain? At age 17, why do I have to bury my child? Why me? I recall one particular Sunday going to church and seeing the picture of a baby girl in the NICU up on the jumbo screen. She was the newborn baby of another young lady at my church who was slightly younger than me at the time. Her baby was suffering from severe complications after birth and the church was asked to go up in prayer for this little baby to survive. I hurt for this mother and I hurt for myself at the same time. I wished they had done this for me. I felt vulnerable and alone like no one had cared enough. It was already embarrassing that I ruined my future and put a stain on my family, now I must bear the burden of loss. A loss that felt like everyone had already forgotten. I held on to that pain for a long time and I let it hold me back from so much. At that time, it probably held me back more than if my son had lived. I had directed my purpose into being someone's mother and now I felt I had no purpose. I smiled in the face of anyone who unknowingly would ask when I had the baby or how my baby was doing. Always finding some way to choke back the tears, I would explain away the situation as to not make them feel uncomfortable or awkward.

Outside of my son's funeral with family and a few close friends, I made a concerted effort to never let anyone see me cry. Up until that day, none of my friends had ever seen me cry. I felt crying in the eyes of others was the wrong thing to do as I shouldn't be sad for something or someone that wasn't supposed to be. But in private, I cried, and this lasted for months. I cried when I looked at his blanket on the pile of clothes I had waiting for him to wear after the day I would bring him home. I cried every time I felt the phantom movements inside me. I cried after waking up from the same recurring dream of my baby crying out for me. I cried if I simply heard the word baby. I cried at baby commercials or whenever I saw a pregnant woman. I cried any time my mother told me it was going to be okay. I cried so much I thought I would drown in my own tears. It turned into a deep depression that no one was able to get me out of. Anger and resentment consumed me. I struggled with trying to finish high school as I fell so far behind and spent most of my time engaged with the only person, I thought could understand what I was feeling as we shared a common tragedy. I felt like a failure and chased after the wrong thing instead of healing myself the right way. At some point, we both outgrew that co-dependent relationship and I no longer could let opportunities to turn my life around pass me by.

I returned to church and this return felt different. I had found a "real-relationship" as I like to call it, with God. It was my own. It wasn't the relationship that your mother or father forced on you every Sunday. It was that deep understanding that you would hear the seasoned generation speak of. I found the kind of relationship that gives you a peace like no other, and it sincerely had me excited to wake up every day to speak with God. I was able to take in and appreciate the little things that I had easily taken for granted while being able to find the lesson in every situation. My story became a story for many young girls who had felt like their mistakes had superseded them. I felt like a child of God who was still deserving of his love and I had not felt that way in a long time.

At age 19 with no high school diploma, I obtained my GED after moving to New York. The idea was to start over in a new environment with new opportunities, go to college and start the path towards that law career, but it didn't work out that way. I wanted to believe that I deserved to win, but I never forgave myself for making poor decisions. I combated with inner fear of failing again and I settled. I settled for working a low wage job and being looked over for not having a college degree. I struggled with the idea of mediocrity; but I accepted it as I felt this was the punishment I was owed. I didn't have a plan for myself, but God did.

I was reminded my value was not lost and my mistakes were forgiven, and they didn't define who I was. There were countless times I was reminded of His forgiveness throughout my life. I was placed in a space during a time that would allow me to demonstrate who God created me to be. He surrounded me with people every step of the way who contributed to my successes no matter how painful. There were times I wanted to quit when the challenge was too tough, and I didn't understand why I had been chosen for the task at hand. At times I didn't feel qualified as it didn't make sense to me how I was able to achieve certain levels of elevation. But I had learned to lean on an understanding that could not be outdone. I recall hearing God say, "I have not forgotten you and I will give you what you thought you lost. Put your trust in me." I have done just that as my journey was my cross to bear. It is not who I am, but it is a part of what I am. It wasn't always easy, and I suffered countless moments of regret and pain, but I didn't let it break me. I eventually learned to stop beating myself with my mistakes and give myself credit for the work I had put in. I weathered my storm and allowed myself the time to heal. The bounce-back allowed me to forgive myself and finally be free of guilt and shame.

"Fear not, for I have redeemed you; I have summoned you by name; you are mine.
When you pass through the waters, I will be with you; and when you pass through the rivers, they will not sweep over you. When you walk through the fire, you will not be burned; the flames will not set you ablaze.
For I am the LORD, your God, the Holy One of Israel, your Savior"

~ Isaiah 43: 1-3 (NIV)

I now know that what was... is not what is.

CHAPTER SEVEN

LIVING LIFE ABUNDANTLY AND FILLED WITH EVERLASTING JOY

ERICA M. BATES

PRELUDE

Have you ever found yourself lacking joy during challenging times or strength to endure during hardships? In uncertain times, you can discover ways that God has provided for you to move from a place of weakness to a place of strength. As a result of challenging times in my life, I would often become upset, angry, or experience spiraling emotions. During these circumstances, I had to fight against developing roots of anger, bitterness, and unforgiveness. These moments are when we need comfort, strength, and encouragement. When God becomes your gardener, He removes the rotten roots of anger, bitterness, and unforgiveness. Then, He comforts, restores, and heals the broken places. Isaiah 51:3 states, "Indeed, Yahweh will comfort Zion, restore her, and comfort all her broken places. He will transform her wilderness into the garden of Bliss, her desert into the garden of Yahweh. Joy and laughter will fill the air with thanksgiving and joyous melodies."

During a time when I had to find joy and strength, God showed me how tending a garden could connect me with the Ultimate Gardener who would become the source of my joy, comfort, encouragement, and strength. My hope is that you discover similar strengths and tools to equip you in uncertain times. Like John in the New Testament, I am writing these things so that you will be filled with the Joy of the Lord. Yes! Remember that your joy will overflow (John 15:11).

...

Encouragement, strength, and joy comes from the Lord. These qualities emerge when a person is rooted in God and in His word. Living without God leads you to a life of anger, bitterness, and unforgiveness. During my senior year of undergraduate school, I applied to several graduate schools to obtain my master's degree in speech pathology. I was excited about taking my next steps in my career and imagined working in a hospital with children as they overcame their challenges. After I received rejection letter after rejection letter, I was hurt and angry.

Later, an opportunity arose to attend a local university on a probationary basis. I believed something would blossom from this. When the semester was complete, one of the professors sat with me in his office and told me that I did not have the aptitude or the knowledge to succeed in a graduate-level program. Crushed! Rejected! I felt angry and disappointed. Yet, when God becomes your gardener, He removes the rotten roots of anger, bitterness, and unforgiveness. The physical act of gardening provided spiritual insight toward the recognition of how God would take me through a process of healing and restoration from negative attitudes and behaviors.

The action of planting and observing plants grow provided me with a glimpse of the value of God's presence and His Word. Keep in mind that my garden consisted of potted plants on my balcony. One of these plants started off strong. Four beautiful green stems flourished with an abundance of green leaves. From the window, the plant appeared amazing with the green leaves contrasting the colorful flowerpot. I watched and waited for the flowers to bloom with the beautiful lilies that I witnessed last summer. However, the heat, dry air, and the rough storms seemed to overwhelm and stress the plant. As time passed, the leaves withered and died. All that was left were tall brown stalks. The flowers failed to bloom. The plant had the potential to transform into something more, yet it produced nothing. The rotten roots of the plant hindered the flower from blooming. Bitterness and anger have the same effect on our spiritual lives. As a result of failing to attend graduate school, bitterness had the potential to take root in my heart. Where there is bitterness, there is no joy. Through this season, I had to remember that Jesus came to remove my anger and bitterness and replace it with joy.

Receiving His joy and accessing His living water means putting ourselves in a position to receive. The acrostic for JOY provided me with a tool to remember to be in a position to receive His joy. J—Join Him in His presence. O—Obtain a lifestyle that is continuously connected to the vine. Y—Yield to His guidance and direction while letting go of negative attitudes.

Joy – In His Presence

Joy is a gift that God brings into our lives like fruit that appears on trees. Joy is not happiness that is based on the situation. Joy is sustainable, renewable, and everlasting. We must hunger, thirst, and crave for His presence consistently. I had to act as if without His presence I would wither and cease to thrive. For without His presence, the watering of the Holy Spirit, we will dry out and deteriorate. Isaiah 35:10 states, "those the LORD has rescued will return. They will enter Zion with singing; everlasting joy will crown their heads. Gladness and joy will overtake them, and sorrow and sighing will flee away."

Eventually, because of God's healing grace my sorrow over not attending graduate school faded and was replaced with a joy of teaching. Oh, how I love to teach! The joy came as I was reading a story to a room full of preschool students and a sudden delight and joy filled my spirit. Joy is found in His presence, everlasting joy. Joy is a decision that I make as I trust in Him. Joy allows me to get over the bitterness and resentment. Joy brings healing and strength. Strength to endure during the night season and to move forward through the storms. Even when weeping endures during the night season, God's joy breaks through the darkness. Joy comes in the morning because Jesus is the light. From Psalm 30:5b, God promises that "the nights of crying your eyes out give way to days of laughter." Putting Him first, drawing near to God, practicing seeking out His presence, being still and listening so God can speak, and praying without ceasing produces the fruit of the spirit. In His presence, there is fullness of Joy.

While the first plant, which was an outdoor plant failed to bloom, one of my indoor plants was transferred outdoors. Inside the house, the plant was warm and cozy. Now outside, the plant had to weather the storms, heat, and lack of water. During my career, God plucked me out of a comfortable situation and moved me into a place that was new, uncomfortable, and challenging. Watching how the leaves and stem of this plant became thinner and dry, reminded me of God's process of transitioning. The dark green stems faded and formed a grayish tone. At certain points, I was uncertain that it would survive. Yet, I recognized how it was becoming stronger and tougher. The stems grew in length and width. Other stems began to slowly sprout from the original stem. Throughout the process, it endured, persevered, and prospered. The stems hardened against the rough weather and became stronger against the wind and the rain. The plant became a vibrant and flourishing organism. From my experiences, I grew in my leadership skills and my spiritual walk with the Lord. Similar to the plant, growth occurs for us when we are connected to the vine. We may feel the winds of personal storms. During challenging times when we harbor unforgiveness, we become hardened and bitter. However, when we receive Jesus and allow His joy to replace unforgiveness, we will begin to flourish. I flourished in my career in education and became a leader, mentor, and trainer in the community.

O - Obtain A Lifestyle That Is Continuously Connected To The Vine

Psalm 30:5 states it this way, "I've learned that His anger lasts for a moment, but His loving favor lasts a lifetime! We may weep through the night, but at daybreak, it will turn into shouts of ecstatic joy." Daybreak comes. Daybreak came when I walked across the stage to receive my master's in education. How does daybreak come? It comes by being connected to the vine. Joy comes due to connectedness to the vine. As I abide in Him, He will abide in me, and I will bear much fruit. Joy is a fruit that grows when I am planted in His word and truth. His joy becomes my joy. Good fruit is produced when there is a connection to the vine. I examine my fruit to determine how well I am connected. John 15:4b -5 says, "You can't bear fruit unless you are joined with me." We bear good fruit when we are connected to Him. Abundant harvest comes when we are joined with the vine so that what we ask for will be listened to and acted upon. A daily dose of studying and memorizing His word, places the Word deep within our hearts. I fill my mind with the Word of God, so my mind is anchored in the truth! The truth that stems from God's Word will set us free. Jesus came so that we can walk in freedom. Free from our spiraling emotions, free from sickness, free from depression, anger, bitterness, and loneliness. Free!

The third plant conveyed the impression that it preferred the outdoor environmental conditions. The flowers and the leaves swayed in the wind and soaked up the sunrays. The plant prospered in the good weather and persevered through the storms. I noticed that whenever the leaves were thirsty from the lack of water, the leaves slumped down and drooped. It appeared sad and gloomy. This reminded me of the times when I felt sad and gloomy. The slumping indicated to me that it was time to water the plant. As soon as the leaves soaked up the water, the plant perked up and stood straight. Water gave it life. The plant needed a constant source of water. It was dependent on the water to survive. I wondered if it had a continuous stream of water would it ever slump over or continually remain straight and vibrant? Creating a continuous source of water allowed this plant to flourish. In times of sadness, I have to reconnect with the source of my joy. What makes a Christ-follower survive through the storms and another fail to succeed? I had to yield my dreams of graduate school to God's direction and timing. Yielding to the leading of the Holy Spirit allows the hurt in our hearts to be healed. We can yield our disappointments and anger over to God and He will replace those negative attitudes.

Y- Yield To His Guidance And Direction While Letting Go Of Negative Attitudes

By allowing His Word to guide, teach, and correct us, we can avoid doubt, jealousy, envy, anger, unforgiveness, fear, and disappointment. In the waiting, plant the seeds of joy, peace, love, grace, and unity by worshipping, serving, and loving God and others. In the hard moments, I choose to sow righteousness by changing my negative thought patterns so that I can reap a plentiful harvest in the waiting. We will reap what we sow. In Matthew 25, the parable of 10 virgins showed me how to be wise and prepare my heart to receive direction from the Lord. The wise virgins were prepared by carrying lamps and oil. In the waiting, how do we greet the Lord? My heart must be submitted to His ways. Each day we have to prepare for His presence, direction, and correction. The wise ones had oil in their lamps and an abundance in their jars.

I ask myself, "What is my thought process?" "Are my words and actions reflecting an upward or downward spiral?" The harvest does not come if we do not plant seeds of truth and are not prepared. I practice letting go of negative attitudes and thoughts so that I can fill myself with God's presence, wisdom, and power. As I attended my postgraduate classes, I had to change my negative thought process to "God has given me the strength and the skill to succeed." When I felt anxious or inadequate to complete the task, I would listen to praise and worship music to fill me with the peace of God.

As a gardener, I was to provide plants with water and nutrients so they would not thirst. Consistently, watering the plants allowed the plants to avoid suffering. God is a constant source, our living water who fills us with His love, hope, and encouragement. Romans 15:13 states, "May the God of hope fill you with all joy and peace as you trust in him, so that you may overflow with hope by the power of the Holy Spirit." From Him, we will never thirst again. Our Father, the ultimate gardener, provides us with what we need each day without hesitation, wondering, questioning, or speculating. Joy, strength, and encouragement emanates from Him and Him alone.

Living a life abundantly is designing a life that is meaningful, purposeful, and joyful. I know that there is an abundant harvest in the waiting. As I attend graduate school to receive my doctorate in education, I know that the abundant harvest is near. I cannot wait. I hold to the promise that "For the Lord, your God will bless you in all your harvest and in all the work of your hands, and your joy will be complete," (Deuteronomy 16:15).

CHAPTER EIGHT

NO, I AM NOT DONE, LAUGHING YET

SEAN SIMMONS

PRELUDE

When you're on your way, getting to where you're going, sometimes you must change from who you are to who you are meant to be along the way. Who you were may not be able to survive in the environment where you're going. That's what I say to myself when I look back at my journey and where I have come from and through my experiences traveling, getting to where I have come and I thank God for the comedy.

...

In Proverbs 17:22 it reads that a joyful heart is good medicine, but a crushed spirit dries up the bones. Seemingly paralyzed by the overwhelming smell of a freshly waxed floor mixed with the smell of paint as if they were both power sprayed up my nostrils, I entered the mustard brown building for my first day at my new school. The sound of lockers slamming mixed with the sound of talking and laughter fill the hallways as I push through the crowd to locate the principal's office on my first day of school. The energy was almost too much as it seemed to make everyone a little jovial which is something I despised at this age. Ugh, school.

"Excuse me, do you know where the principal's office is?" I asked, knowing I did not care one bit about those directions.

Her hair laid over her right shoulder as I read her every move seemingly missing the words, she was saying. "Thank you."

"What floor is this?" I said, hoping this conversation could continue forever.

April was a junior in school and was the only person who made me feel like I belong there. Ring...ring.

"Nice meeting you," she said as she walked off to her class.

She almost made me forget what I was doing. Oh yeah, the principal's office. Little did I know, I would be spending a lot of time here. They should call this my office.

Huh...Huh! Deeper breaths, adrenaline surging, heart pounding loud enough to drown out all the people yelling, screaming, and pushing to see a fight. I can't lose this one…if I lose this, I lose more than just an image or an ego boost. Come on Sean…I have to get it together, I tell myself, wanting the torment to end. The visceral nature of anger begins to manifest, fueling an explosive chain reaction throughout my body causing me to launch a counterattack after feeling a large gust of wind brush my left cheek. Another failed swarm of blows coming close enough to fracture my face. I really think he's mad.

Crack! My accuracy seemed good enough to target his right eye with an overhand left, but it was bad enough to catch the bottom of his jawline knocking him to the ground, a few more and he'll be done.

"Where is my book bag?"

Hands burning. That's funny. His face felt soft when I was punching it. Man, my hands hurt! Then a stinging sensation begins to numb my face as I walk home from another normal day of high school.

The scent of fresh cut grass fills the rainy air, and the clouds were as grey as any bad day could muster for my worst day in school history.

Why did I have to open my big mouth?

"Nice open-toe steel-toes…who wears sandals?" I said.

My friends and I quickly bend the corner hurrying to a block where the gang activity isn't as prevalent, judging by the graffiti tagging all over the fences and street signs. Hurrying like someone leaving a crime scene...cause that's what you do when you don't want to be at the scene of any crime...you leave. I make my way home after saying goodnight to the last of my friends as I check my pockets finally locating my keys. My mom would kill me if I lost this key again. I enter, hoping that there aren't any scars that my mom can give me a whooping for. It had to be a lot worse for people who lose a fight and then go home to get punished.

Even years later, I laugh at how blessed I was to find a way to use comedy to befriend my bullies after I beat most of them up. I wasn't a troublesome child. I just thought that being funny was a way to make friends. I didn't know that it is also the fastest way to make a whole bunch of enemies. But I learned that really quickly! I couldn't think of a joke funny enough to make many friends until after I left high school...even now I still seem to struggle.

My conscious belief is that we need comedy to release tension as mental, social, and psychological pressure builds from friction caused by everyday experiences. Everyday friction can be as little as trying to understand why my keys aren't where I left them while running late for a meeting to going to jail because you hit something with your car while mad/angry because you were late for that same meeting. The point is, don't sweat the little stuff and learn to laugh at yourself. Laughter can be the one thing that saves someone from making a mistake that they would have to live with for the rest of their lives.

Using comedy to stay motivated comes from sharpening your joke/laughter muscle in a way to help guard or promote a mood or mindset. Being seasoned in the art of controlling one's energy, comedy can help defend against some of the most oppressive or experiences brought on by an adversarial presence. Have you ever heard the saying, "Laugh to keep from crying" or the saying "I cried laughing?" Staying on task to accomplish your goals is the only thing that will truly keep you from crying; laughter just makes the journey fun and memorable on the way.

I remember as I grew older and eventually had kids that I finally heard God speaking into my life. It was a beautiful Saturday morning that I was working out in the basement with my oldest son, who was only about three years old at the time. While I was completing my 1,000,000th push up (that's right ladies), I noticed that it was about time for me to set him on the potty because we were potty training him. After I set him on the potty in front of the TV, I heard a knock at the door. Wondering whom it could be, I heard another knock and told my son I would be back shortly, stay on the potty. As I reached the top of the stairs, I thought that maybe I should grab some water since I wanted to complete another 100,000 push-ups. After grabbing the water from the fridge, the job of opening the front door was finally here. Two men dressed in white button up short sleeve shirts and some color-stricken tie were standing at the door. Humor quickly entered my mind as I contemplated the many ways possible to enjoy, tease, harass these men who were here to witness to me. Or so they thought.

I opened the door and immediately shut the door while they were talking in an attempt to reach the highest amount of rudeness possible in the beginning of our conversation. I don't want them to get spoiled and think that I'm actually listening when things get more heated in about 15 mins later. I let it be known at the beginning that this is the type of behavior they would receive throughout the entire conversation.

After explaining to them that Jesus is a black man, my son came up the stairs and said, "Daddy."

"Yes."

"Are you doing okay?"

There is an overwhelming feeling of joy when a father hears his firstborn say the words daddy. Around that time, it still freaked me out whenever he talked like he wanted to have a conversation. There he stood with his green shirt, white socks, and in his hand, he had the diaper I took off of him when I set him on the potty. He is standing there holding the diaper filled with booboo. I can't believe it. He smeared it all the way up the stairs on the walls and what seemed to be everywhere. After closing the door on our guest for the last and final time, we rushed downstairs so I could put him back on the mickey mouse potty we got from Target and go back over our former plan of action. As I set him back down, I saw all the mess he made that I was going to have to clean up and I started to get mad. As I got mad at my son, knowing I was wrong, I began to pray. I began to pray and ask God to help me so that I would be a good father and raise my kids right.

As I was praying, I felt someone tap me on my forehead. Opening my eyes, I can still remember seeing that small little finger slowly moving back from my head. A little baby finger with poop on it. No!!! Get it off me! Get it off me! Ugh... I knew right then, at that moment, that God was laughing at me.

I still remember the Jehovah witness from that day whenever reminiscing on how God has brought me through. I leave you with this powerful Scripture that has changed my life. In Proverbs 17:22 it reads, "A Joyful heart is good medicine, but a crushed spirit dries up the bones." Using comedy to stay motivated is good, but how do you stay on task and not get distracted when using comedy to stay motivated? Well, you're going to have to check out our next book on staying on task when using comedy to stay motivated. Snippet: "Mr. Simmons, could you please step up out of the car you're under arrest. Please step out of the vehicle and put your hand behind your back. I will not tell you again."

"Why is this happening to me, is what I ask myself as I turn the key and reach to unlock my seat belt."

PRAYER

Father I pray that as we learn to laugh more, that you will begin to do the work of healing in us. Help us to put our trust in you, so we worry less about things that don't matter. Help us to see and to enjoy all that you have already done for us and in us. Help us to utilize laughter for healing and to rely upon you for peace. In Jesus Name, Amen.

CHAPTER NINE

INNER ENCOURAGEMENT

CEOLA CHARLES

PRELUDE

It started years ago. Growing up from a child to becoming an adult, I have always depended on my parents for spiritual and moral guidance. Every time I asked my dad or mom for advice, there would always be a word from his favorite Bible quote that provided me direction for whatever I was going through. My dad would remind me, "All things work together for the good to them that love the Lord. For I am persuaded, that neither death, nor life, nor angels, nor principalities, nor powers, nor things present, nor things to come, nor height, nor depth, nor any other creature, shall be able to separate us from the love of God, which is in Christ Jesus our Lord," (Romans 28:28-30). Although my father's Bible recitations, pontifications, or his preaching actually got on my nerves at times as a child, I learned that knowing and taking the Scripture literally is sufficient in itself to motivate and support me through trials and adversities. There truly is not anything that can separate us from the love of God, for He is a loving God.

...

To give encouragement to others has always been one of my passions. I've always been told that I have the gift of encouragement, if there is such a thing. I just love helping people and motivating them to be their best, and I believe that is something that I got from my parents, the late Bishop Alpheus and Olive Williams. They showed love to each person they met and always listened to God when He guided them to help and encourage those on their path. My mom was the women's missionary leader. God would use her to minister to women in need and always give her the words to encourage them. I would often hear her speaking to and uplifting the women in church. However, encouragement came not just in words but in deeds. I remember my dad had a garden outside on a portion of land. People would come to church hungry, and he would have them fill their bags with fresh vegetables, while my mom would bake bread and take it to church to pass out fresh loaves and rolls to members. That was how ministry was instilled in me by my parents. They were my examples of how to love and minister to people and I now understand today how it is a part of my purpose

Growing up in church all my life, serving and trusting in the Word of God, there were lots of good times and some not so good times. When I was 18 years old, I got married and immediately afterward, my husband and I started a family. Soon we had four children, two girls and two boys, and each one a blessing. Life moved along so quickly even back then but my ultimate passion of serving and making people smile remained the same. I love my family so much and I just wanted to make sure everyone around me was good, so I always put their needs before myself. Throughout my marriage I experienced infidelity and some hurtful situations in my life and found the only thing I could do was cry and pray and pray and pray. During some of those difficult times, I had an out-of-body experience that was so amazingly beautiful I knew it was God's way of letting me know that He was there the entire time and caring for me. My spirit left my body for a short period of time while I was actually sitting in my car. I saw myself sitting there and my spirit said to myself, "If anyone would see me, they would say I'm dead." When my spirit returned to my body, a song came out of nowhere... from the cd or the radio...

"Take up your cross and live for Jesus

If you're in doubt, there is no reason
Read the word and live for Jesus
Then you will have eternal life."
~ the L.A Mass Choir

From that experience, I was reminded that God was with me and knew He was real in my life.

After several years of being unhappy and feeling like I needed a change, I relocated to the east coast and when I got settled, I then had to restructure my life. After being married for so many years, focusing on cooking what my husband wanted to eat and taking care of him and the children, it was interesting to think about what my new life would look like and what my goals, passion, and purpose was. I was always that person to kind of do what other people wanted me to do, and just go along with the decisions made. Even when we watched television, my husband had the remote and I literally watched whatever he wanted. I had no problem with it being all about my husband and my children as I loved them dearly, however, when I moved, I had to figure out what I wanted and needed. Even though too many times I felt like I didn't deserve it, I knew that God's desire is for his children to be happy and fulfilled, and that just living as a daughter of the King meant there are certain rights and privileges that I'd been given. Still, it took me years to figure out and embrace that by His grace, I did in fact deserve God's best.

Fast forward twenty plus years later, after being separated from my husband for a time, we finalized our divorce. The day it was finalized I felt something that I couldn't explain, but it seems ironic how you marry someone and later down the road you get divorced. After a while of trying to gain an understanding, I realized how marriage was a spiritual bond and connection, and that bond being severed with my husband was painful. All I could do was take advantage of standing on the Word of God, encourage myself, and trust God to bring me through, and that He did. As the songwriter Marvin Sapp wrote,

"When I look back over all You brought me through
I can see that You were the one I held on to
And I never would have made it without You."

Thinking back over my life, if I could do life all over again there are things that I would not change. My four amazing children from my marriage have all grown up to be talented, gifted, and such incredible individuals. My two boys are now strong young men, and my two girls are extraordinary young women, all of them are awesome entrepreneurs doing remarkable things, and I am proud beyond words of who they are today. I give all the glory and praise to the Almighty Father for He has truly brought me through, and I "never would've made it" without Him. This song along with many others became a part of my testimony. The words lit a fire inside of me and gave me the courage to continue to be all that I was placed on this earth to be. My heart was, and is still to serve, and I find that God always opens doors for me to minister to His people.

Ever since I relocated, God has allowed me to serve in multiple ministries. Currently I am a part of an amazing church in which I serve in the music department. I love my pastors, Drs. Mike and Deedee Freeman, and appreciate them for continuing to encourage me to hear God and minister to the needs of people around me. The Lord continues to bless me with opportunities along my path to talk to and pray for people all the time; to help people who are in need and to encourage them whether on an airplane sitting next to a stranger, or in the grocery store.

I walked in the FedEx store one day and asked the lady who waited on me how she was doing. She proceeded to tell me she had a pain in her arm for months.

At that moment I knew the Lord had placed her in my path for a reason so I told her, "I would like to pray for you if that's okay."

She bowed her head, and I began to pray. While praying for her I felt the Holy Spirit moving. Since I know that God is a healer and I was taught to trust and obey Him, I believe that the Lord healed her, and just like that, I left it in His hands! As I walked away, I felt my release.

Every job that I have worked has also been a platform for ministry. One position I held for many years was in customer service. As a phone representative with a bank, I would get phone calls from people having challenges with the money held in the financial institution. There was this particular lady that was in tears and frantically began to ask for what she needed. As she spoke, I could hear the Spirit of the Lord giving me each word to minister to her. I told her everything was going to be okay and I was able to service her and minster to her at the same time.

I believe if everyone looked at their jobs as places to show the love of God and to be His hands and feet the world would be a better place today. If everyone just simply encouraged one person who crossed their path, imagine how much better life would be. These are my few words to say that through it all, I learned to trust the Lord and His Word, for He is my inner encouragement that keeps my passion to encourage others ignited. With that being said, I want to encourage you. God's got you and is going to see you through every challenge, rough road, and obstacle! It won't always be easy but just know that He has your back.

PRAYER

Heavenly Father, I pray for each and every one who needs to be encouraged today. Lord send people with the right words to speak over them. Help them to stand on Your Word and to follow after You as never before. Lift them up and help them to see that they belong to You...in the mighty Name of Jesus...Amen.

CHAPTER TEN

A WEEKEND TO REMEMBER

VALERIA LATIMORE

PRELUDE

"If a rose can grow through a crack in the pavement
Should I falter or waiver on days when nothing's going
right, and I feel everything has gone wrong
I will think of the mustard seed and continue to stand
strong. For thou art with me."

~ L. Dawson

•••

It was a cool day in November, the year of 2005. My daughter's teacher called me informing me that she was telling him off in front of the classroom which had alarmed me because she was actually my mild-tempered daughter. This happened to be on a Friday, so when she arrived home from school, I was ready to discipline her, and in doing so I noticed how she would hastily go from being silly to having an attitude, but I attributed that to her being a teenager. My daughter was fourteen years old, in the ninth grade, and one of the star basketball players, so you can imagine my confusion from her reaction of laughter as I discussed with her the conversation her teacher and I had. Her abnormal reaction to the situation led me to worry because her behavior was a reflection and remembrance of my past teenage life of which I had been warned about before it actually took place. If you've heard of or experienced any of the teenager and parent chronicles, you're feeling my despair as you read and can picture me very afraid. Needless to say, my daughter was grounded.

The weekend moves forward, and I notice my daughter is being very clumsy. She's stumbling over things and she even fell in the laundry basket. I'm thinking in my mind that she's working really hard to get off this punishment and I wasn't even trying to hear all that nor was I having that. I tell her If she doesn't straighten up, I'm gonna give her more than a punishment. Y'all know what she was headed for. Yep, a behind whooping fit for a fourteen-year-old. In doing all these things, she just thought everything was so funny, but promised me that she wasn't doing them on purpose. I'm clearly getting tired of her acting this way at this point and on top of that I keep getting this worried feeling in the pit of my stomach. Later I will find out that feeling was the Holy Spirit giving me a warning as well as strengthening me for what was to come.

The weekend ended and Monday morning came. I went in to wake my daughter for school which wasn't normal because she's always on point and precise with everything that she does. She's never late for anything, including school. She got up and was moving kind of sluggishly. I'm still feeling uneasy, but still just don't know what it is. She gets dressed, heads to the bus stop, and goes to school. She finishes up her day and when she comes home, she's extremely tired, so she naps and then does her chores, homework, and the rest of her responsibilities. The week goes on and I'm noticing she's looking kind of different. So being a woman of faith, I beef my prayer up for her. Now I was raised straight Holiness Pentecostal, so you know this prayer consisted of oil slanging and demon terminating power, to say the least. At the same time, I'm talking to my daughter trying to see if she's met new friends or talking on the phone to new people or if something has happened to her emotionally or physically that I wasn't aware of because I just knew something wasn't right.

Friday comes and by this time my daughter is limping and her hand looks a little funny, so I'm really concerned, but I must tell the truth. I'm also in denial. I know my daughter isn't sick, she can't be. She's so weak that she took an extremely long time getting dressed. I even dropped her off at school because she missed the bus. Now after I get in the car, I just start bawling crying on my way to work. It bothered me so bad I called my husband and asked him to go check her out of school and take her to the hospital. I'm going on about my day, I get to my afternoon clients and then I get *the* phone call. My husband is on the other end and he tells me to sit down. Well, I'm already sitting down because I'm doing nails I tell him. I am not expecting what he's about to tell me. He begins to tell me that my daughter is very sick, and we are going to have to rush her to Birmingham where the specialists are. I'm trying to keep my composure at this point. He says that they gave her an MRI and the results showed that she had a brain tumor of which had taken up 60% of the right side of her brain. I let out a holler so strong and loud that my receptionist rushed from the front of the salon to check on me. There she found me on the floor. I instructed her to cancel all my appointments for the weekend, and the lady in the chair, God bless her, my receptionist, had to finish her topcoat and she must have done a decent job because the client continued to come.

I rushed to the hospital and to my surprise when I walked in my daughter was calm. By that time, she was almost completely paralyzed on her entire left side. When I saw her face and noticed how she was being so strong, I dried up my tears immediately and my "faithdometor" kicked into extra high gear. My daughter began to confess about some things that she had gotten entangled in that she knew were not pleasing to God. She informed me that she repented unto God and she is believing Isaiah 53:5. Now she's fourteen y'all. If you train them up in the way, they should go...God's promises are true every time.

Moving forward, the doctors are now asking me if I want her to go to Birmingham by ambulance or if I want to take her myself. Either way she has to go because Montgomery health systems weren't equipped to help her. I chose to take her myself because I had some business to take care of. My cousin drove us. May God bless him forever for that one. When I tell you, I laid hands on my daughter from Montgomery all the way to Birmingham. Now Birmingham was about 115 miles away and by the time we got there I had commanded every system in her body to line up with the Word of God: "By the stripes of Jesus, she is healed, and she will not only walk but she will play basketball again."

As we arrive at The Children's Hospital, they begin checking us in and running their tests and such. The verdict comes back that it was indeed a tumor and was also causing the paralysis. They said by the looks of it she would need brain surgery. I can remember looking for tears and only having one lonely tear coming down my face every day. This was something to deal with, but God's strength is definitely perfect and it kicks in when you need it the most. At this point we were believing God, but we needed more strength, so I called in the prayer warriors. You all know what happens when the fervent effectual prayer goes forth. I could have danced right then and there. Thank You Jesus!! They begin to get her prepped for surgery as they tell us the pros and cons of the procedure. One con was that she may not ever walk again, and I just was not going to accept that, and neither was my daughter. So, the prayer warriors began to pray, and you know what happens when we pray. The atmosphere in my daughter's hospital room was saturated with the presence of God that when the surgeon came in, he asked had we been praying. I asked him why. He said that he could just tell.

My daughter gets all prepped and ready for surgery and all of a sudden, the surgeon says that he just feels that he should take another MRI. We go down to take the test. My daughter is claustrophobic so she does not want this MRI done, and in order to make her feel better, she wants me to hold her hand and pull her sock half way off of one of her feet. You must know that the sock had basketballs all over it. The results come back and to the doctor's surprise he sees something different about her brain. He comes in the room and starts to use all of these medical terms and I stop him because all I'm hearing is the tumor is shrinking, and to confirm, I ask him is that what he's telling us.

He says, "Yes," with a huge smile on his face.

I told him that's all I wanted to hear. He goes on to say that she no longer had to have the surgery.

We didn't know exactly what the cause was. First, they said seizure, but that didn't check out. Then they said multiple sclerosis, but the thing about the MS is when you have a breakdown with that, the indentions on your brain are known to be permanent. I was never at peace about that diagnosis, so we prayed some more. Mind you at this point Shylanda's back home. She was only at the hospital for about a week because she was progressing so fast. The neurologist was actually surprised to see her progression coming along so quickly when we went to have an MRI after her release. The physical therapist was even impressed. Shylanda's faith was very high and she was determined to walk, play sports, and be independent again. She worked very hard I must say. She even did brain work. What I mean by that is she didn't want to graduate late because of her situation, but it was hard to do her work because this involved her brain. I told her to read every day and she did. Needless to say, she passed every class with flying colors.

It was time for a visit to read her MRI and see exactly what was going on. We go in and the doctor begins to pull it up on the screen where we all can see. He's telling me how I need to prepare for her having these episodes because once it's there, it's pretty much irreversible. To all of our surprise, when the image comes up the tumor reveals that it's shrinking, and not only is it shrinking but it's shrinking at a rapid speed. I immediately started giving God praise!! My daughter totally recovered. She played basketball on her high school team and was actually a starting point guard. She went to college and currently owns several businesses. This was totally a faith experience for our family to grow. Now we know for a fact what will happen if we believe God's word. No matter how dim it may look, always believe the truth instead of the fact.

CHAPTER ELEVEN

PAIN THERAPY

ADRIENNE VARLACK

PRELUDE

"God is our refuge and strength, an ever-present help in trouble. Therefore, we will not fear, though the earth gives way and the mountains fall into the heart of the sea, though its waters roar and foam and the mountains quake with their surging. There is a river whose streams make glad the city of God, the holy place where the Most High dwells. God is within her, she will not fall; God will help her at break of day."

~Psalm 46:1-5

...

Times were hard growing up. We had some good days, and as a family we loved each other, but often money was tight, and our home life was dysfunctional. My mother was the kind of person who made tough situations easier to bear. She had faith like no other person I know. If we didn't know where our next meal was coming from, she would say, "God will provide," and shortly after someone would come knocking on our door with a bag of food. Or, if we were afraid, she would say, "God has not given us the spirit of fear," and her words would comfort us. She took God's word to heart and taught us to do the same. But when you're a child and things are bad at home it is difficult to believe they can ever get better.

In all of this, I somehow got it in my head that if I behaved as a *good girl* and did everything *just right*, then the bad would go away. But it never happened. Instead, as I grew, so did the severity of our struggles. And as the eldest child, I made it my job to try and keep the peace. So, I had to try even harder to do my best and to be extra good, all the while thinking that my *personal goodness* would make the pain and chaos in my life stop.

So, I decided to start a campaign of good deeds. I ministered to the young women at our church. I went out into the community and witnessed to my neighbors. I taught Sunday school. I mean how much more of a *good* girl could I be? Surely now things would change for the better! What I didn't realize was that the pain and struggle in my life was actually strengthening my relationship with God.

When I got married, I carried this *good girl* attitude with me. I thought that if I could be a good wife, I would have the perfect marriage. I would love, be loved, and feel loved at all times. But, as life would have it, my husband

and I had our share of troubles. Through it all, I clung to my core belief: If I am good, things will change. Besides, trials only came to make me strong right? So, I prayed to God and just kept trying to be strong.

As the years passed, God blessed us with two beautiful children, and I thought that I had finally received my reward for being a good girl. I was so very happy and anything else I was going through did not matter as I filled my life with my children.

It wasn't until I had my third child that I realized the trials I had gone through in life could not compare to what was about to happen. In fact, those hard times were preparing me for a season of pain I would almost not recover from. You see, the struggles of my childhood and early on in my marriage taught me to stay on my face before God. The example of a worshipful and prayerful attitude set by my mother in our home stuck with me. As a result, I prayed constantly because I knew that bad things could always be worse. God was teaching me, developing in me encouraging and peaceful habits that would sustain and keep me in this next season.

Shortly after I had my second child, I became pregnant for the third time with my daughter, Andrea. She was the biggest of my three children, and the calmest. Andrea came into the world sleeping through the night. She was kind, loving, and mischievous. Around the age of seven months, I started to notice that when I would feed her, she could not keep anything down. She did not smile as my other children had and did not seem to make the sweet cooing noises that most babies did at that age. Around ten months, her looks started to change and her forehead began to protrude outward. She still looked like my sweet baby girl, but when others began to comment, or ask me what was wrong with her, I decided to take her to a doctor.

The first doctor's report was hard to hear. My baby girl had what was called craniosynostosis. Craniosynostosis is defined by the CDC as a birth defect in which the bones in a baby's skull join too early. This happens before the baby's brain is fully formed. As the baby's brain grows, the skull can become more misshapen. Andrea's condition also caused fluid to form on the brain and this is what was causing her problems with digestion and delayed speech. She needed to have a shunt put in to drain the fluid and then reconstructive surgery to repair skull deformity.

My husband and I were shaken by this diagnosis, but it wasn't fatal. We had our friends and family praying for her, and we believed God for total and complete recovery. The morning of the surgery, we were confident that the procedure would be a success and that Andrea would soon be on the road to recovery. When the nurse took Andrea for a final examination, we were nervous but hopeful.

The examination process was taking a long time and we wondered if they had rushed her to surgery without telling us. As the minutes ticked by, I became increasingly concerned. What seemed to be hours later, the nurse practitioner emerged and stated that he was cancelling the surgery because he wanted a specialist to look at Andrea. He felt that the initial diagnosis may have been incorrect and wanted a pediatric specialist to confirm this before subjecting her to a traumatic surgical procedure. So, he sent her for an x-ray and an MRI, and then sent us home.

I remember being so upset because it was hard waiting for this surgery date to come and this hurdle was supposed to be over by now. Andrea would heal nicely, and we could get back to normal. Or at least, that's what I had been hoping for. In the days that followed, fear began to take a hold on me. I worried about her test results, about all of the awful possibilities, but most of all, I worried about what would come next. Several days later, we were called to the children's hospital to discuss Andrea's test results with the pediatric specialist.

I was so nervous, but I hid it by pretending to be annoyed about waiting for another surgery date. The doctor called my sister and me to an office where he displayed Andrea's X-rays. The doctor told us that the X-rays and blood test indicated that Andrea had a rare genetic disorder called Hurler Syndrome.

"Hurler Syndrome," I thought, "What is that?"

I vaguely remember standing there as the doctor was explaining. But the only thing I can remember clearly from that visit are these words: "There is no cure!"

Those words seemed to echo out of his mouth and just hang there in a bubble like you see in those cartoons. I thought to myself, "Well maybe that is true for others, but not for my child." He went on to explain that there were very few cases in the U.S., and they had very little research to give support. The books tell them that most children die from this disease. I cannot explain the feeling that came over me, hearing that my child may die. I couldn't even cry, though my sister was devastated. All the time I was saying to myself, "God wouldn't put more on me than I can bear." Andrea is going to be one of those stories you hear about on TBN when God does a great miracle—An "everybody thought she wouldn't make it, but she did and look at her now" kind of thing.

After ten months of doctors, nurses, medicine, chemotherapy, a bone marrow transplant, and respirators, my lovely little girl left this world at the age of 20 months. I could not believe that my daughter had died. We had prayed and fasted. We had what seemed like the entire world praying for our child to live. We had Scriptures posted on the wall of her hospital room. My husband would go around to other children's rooms and pray for them with their parents. I mean, come on, we were the model Christians. We deserved a miracle.

The process of planning the funeral, picking out clothing, telling family members, and any and all preparation (I only know about because of what other people have told me), I now know that it was God's way of keeping my sanity. I was so lost. The only thing I really remember is thinking that my God had failed me. But God, in fact, was about to show me just how much He really loved me. As I stated before, there is a lot I don't remember when we finally came home to prepare for her funeral. I'm told that my parents, husband, and his family planned everything. I remember being at the gravesite and leaving my child to be buried. I remember coming home and being in my room where it seemed dark all the time. My husband says that my mom and sister stayed with us for three months, but I honestly don't remember that at all.

The next thing I remember clearly is the day I woke up. I can't explain it more than that. It just seemed like I was asleep and suddenly I was awake. The pain was unbearable, my arms ached to hold my child and my body ached to nurse her, but I could do neither. I remember sitting at my window and asking God, "Why me? Why did you let this happen to me?"

I heard in my mind, "Why not you? People all over the world experience loss, why do you think you would be exempt?"

With tears of anger, disappointment, and frustration in my eyes, I reminded God that I have always been a good girl. I did what I was supposed to do. I prayed, I believed when others didn't, I've been in ministry for years! I've helped people, been obedient to my parents...all the things I was supposed to do.

I asked, "After all of that, how could you do this to me?"

I heard nothing back.

I said, "Fine, I'm not going to serve you anymore. If all that I endured in my childhood wasn't enough suffering, and all the good things I've done don't mean anything, then what's the point?"

At that moment I was done serving God, but before the moment could pass, I asked myself, "Now what?" My first experience with God was at the age of four. I have literally served the Lord all of my life. What was I supposed to do without Him? In my next breath, I returned to God.

Over the next couple of days, I stayed in my room, sitting on the edge of my bed sobbing. I could hear my husband and children in other rooms of the house living without me, but I could not bring myself to move from that spot. I was concerned by God's silence. Maybe God left me. Maybe I shouldn't have told Him that I wasn't going to serve Him anymore. What have I done? I lost my baby and now I have lost my God.

On one of those days, my husband came into the room and handed me the phone. I don't remember him saying anything. I just took the phone. On the other end I heard a man's voice.

He said to me, "Trecy, God told me to tell you that He sees you sitting in your room in the dark and He hears you crying."

Even though I had been crying in that spot for days, I cried even more at that moment. God heard me. God loves me. God sees me. It was the best news I'd had in months.

That same day I got up off the bed, turned on my room light, and went out to be with my family.

Now, I wish I could tell you that everything was perfect after that, but it wasn't. The pain I felt after losing my daughter was unbearable and tears and outbursts of anger would happen without any warning. I was grieving. I had experienced loss before with family members and close friends, but nothing could compare to the grief I would experience from the loss of a child. I would cry out to God on a daily basis. I tried not to show my children my sadness, but they knew. Even though God assured me that He was with me, there were many times I still felt like He was far away.

On one particular occasion, I cried out to God in my kitchen.

While doubled over I asked, "Lord, why is this happening to me? This feels so bad and nobody knows how I feel God. You don't know how much this hurts!"

And I heard Him say to me loud and clear, "I lost a child too."

Instantly, I stood up straight because those words said to me that the only one who can help me through this process knows exactly how I feel. Hearing His voice gave me strength to keep going.

After this realization, my daily prayer life increased ten-fold. My conversations with God gave me courage to slowly start integrating myself back into daily life. During this time, we relocated to a new church. Two weeks later, God opened the first door to ministry to share my grief. I was introduced to a young woman whose baby was stillborn. My pastor thought it would be a good idea for me to talk to her. I said yes, but in my mind, I was irritated by how inconsiderate his request seemed to be. But I went to see her anyway and when we saw each other, neither of us said a word. We just embraced and cried the entire time we were together. There was a deeper understanding and comfort needed that words could not communicate.

Over the next year and a half, I went through the different stages of grief. I cried and asked God if He was still there. Many times, I questioned why I had to go through such pain. But every time He comforted and reassured me that He loved me, and I was able to go on. God was there every step of the way, sometimes walking beside me and sometimes carrying me, but always there.

Because of this I wanted more of God. I loved to pray and worship and the more I did the more I wanted to. God was giving me the tools to build my strength in Him and as the years went on, I craved more of Him. Here, eighteen years after the death of my child, I love Him more than ever. He never failed me and never left me. I was in so much pain and my Savior never left my side. His promise is that He will never leave us nor forsake us. He never said that if you are good to me, then I will be good to you. No! Sometimes life is so hard you have to pray through tears, sing with your teeth clenched, and love with your fist balled up behind your back. Guess what? God will still love you.

Through all the suffering, he gives me what I need to be encouraged when I feel like I'm alone. When no friend can be found or can understand, He's given me the ability to encourage myself.

There's a line in the song "Defender" sung by Rita Springer, that I love. "When I thought I lost me, You knew where I left me. You reintroduced me to Your love." This is one of my favorite lines in a song because it says to me that even though I felt like I was lost, God knew just where I was. That is because He was with me the whole time. This is the kind of thing God has deposited in me so that I can use it to encourage myself. Is everything perfect? No, but neither am I. That's okay, because I serve the One who is perfect, and He loves me anyway.

PRAYER

Thank you, God, for allowing us to process our grief in a way that is real and true. When it seems like no one understands, You know what we are feeling better than we do and are willing to listen anyway. You use our pain and disappointment as a way to propel us to the next level in You all the while keeping us whole. Help us to see Your master plan, and if we cannot see clearly Lord, help us to trust You at Your word when you declare You will never leave us nor forsake us. Amen

CHAPTER TWELVE

STAND UP!

KATRINA PORTES
(Names changed to protect privacy)

PRELUDE

"Stand up straight and realize who you are, that you
tower over your circumstances... Develop enough
courage so that you can stand up for yourself and then
stand up for somebody else."

~Maya Angelou

. . .

Some of you may remember me as the "Stand-Up" lady
from a video that went viral on FaceBook and other social
media outlets a year ago. Many people found great comic
relief in the video where I spoke to my son from the stage
at my church, telling him to "Stand-up!" in respect and
reverence at an appropriate time in church. It was
relatable. It was nostalgic. Obviously, I wasn't at all
expecting that moment to be captured on video, and most
certainly not expecting it to be watched and commented
on by millions of people. While I could understand how
others found it funny because it was so relatable and took

them back to similar moments in their childhood, it wasn't so funny to me. In fact, it was a pivotal moment in time for my son and I and demonstrative of our relationship in general since the passing of his father, my husband. You see, his father, my junior high school sweetheart and first love, suddenly passed away at the age of 35. As you can probably imagine, it was a tragedy that rocked the foundation of our family, and quite frankly, my faith. My son, Kyle (name changed to protect privacy), was only seven at the time.

That moment in time changed the trajectory of what I saw for our future. And it was a very complex experience to navigate. The grief and complexities of it were very difficult to understand and almost unbearable to process at times. There were suddenly many uncertainties about life for us. Will we ever really get through this? How will we get through this? Will my heart heal? Will our children's hearts heal? What will be our new normal? How will this experience impact our children long-term? Will I ever experience joy again? Those were some of the many questions I would ponder on a daily basis after losing my husband, but one thing that I was certain of was that I had to learn how to be strong for my children and be the best parent I could be despite our circumstances. In that moment, the only thing that kept me from simply giving up was knowing that I was now tasked to continue raising my children to be the most well-rounded, respectable young men, with good morals and values, in the fear and admonition of God.

However, this was no easy feat with Kyle, in particular. After his father passed away, our relationship quickly turned into one of strife and contention, fueled by the grief and anger that we were both newly introduced to. It was the most traumatic experience that any of us had and it was unchartered territory to navigate. I knew that it rocked Kyle, yet he didn't talk much about it. Looking back, I am sure that him internalizing his thoughts and feelings about what had happened exacerbated his anger. But in the moment, I was so focused on how to mitigate the pain for myself, minute to minute, that I didn't place enough emphasis on his pain.

For me, the sadness was overwhelming. I can remember crying every day for two years straight and contemplating and entertaining many unhealthy thoughts. I just didn't feel strong enough to get through *today*, let alone the days ahead. There was constant mental turmoil throughout the night, and from the moment I woke up, it would follow me throughout the day. I spent hours on the road, traveling back and forth to work, and all I could do was think and cry. I often tell people that those first two years felt like there was a constant dark, rainy cloud over my head from the moment I woke up each day until the moment I went to sleep. It relentlessly followed me. Yet, it seemed to be sunshine and blue skies for everyone else, similar to cartoon depictions I recall when I was a child. At least this was my perspective. Each and every day, I did whatever I needed to do that day, just to get through that day.

I know there were many people praying for us. But me, I was angry. And the one thing I wasn't doing was praying. I was angry! I was angry with God first and foremost. The persistent question in my mind was, "Why me?" How could you let this happen to me? This may seem like an insensitive or arrogant question, but it was the only question I would have when I did actually talk to God. Honestly, I had lost my faith. I had always seemed to be protected in my life. I was protected in my childhood, living in a household with two loving parents, never experiencing any childhood trauma. I was protected in my young adult life, never experiencing any trauma while growing into womanhood. I married the love of my life and had beautiful, healthy children. Life for me had always been smooth and I had expected it would always be that way. Then one day, it all suddenly changed in an instant! The protection that I had been used to was stripped away. There were many emotions I felt. There were the usual suspects of initial shock and sadness, and then there were some unsuspecting ones like shame and embarrassment. But when the dust settled, the overarching emotion for me was definitely severe anger. Not only was I angry with God, but I was angry when I saw others leading happy lives. I felt left out. I felt forgotten about. I felt overlooked, disregarded, and discarded.

Initially, all that I did was sit. I can remember sitting on my couch for several weeks, barely moving just to get up and use the restroom, unless I was headed to my bed. In my mind, I had quit my job. I just gave up for a while. I didn't eat and didn't have peaceful sleep. My family, friends, and church family rallied around us. They prayed for us big time and they came around even when I wouldn't speak a word to them. Some would speak soft words of encouragement to me. Others would be brave enough to give me *tough love*, telling me to get myself together, *stand up*, and put one foot in front of the other. Others would just sit in silence with me. They were just...there. I was quiet. I was a recluse.

Kyle's anger showed up in different ways. He didn't say much either, but his actions spoke volumes. I grew accustomed to very regular phone calls home and emails from his teachers and school administrators. They would report everything from failing grades to constant class disruptions to school fights he would be involved in. And none of it was much different from what I was experiencing at home or at church for that matter. If you recall from the video, I had to tell him three times to stand up! It was exhausting. Add this on top of the grief we were already trying to process, and it was a recipe that fueled a conflict-ridden relationship for the two of us. I tried many things to help Kyle. We went through grief counseling. I kept him active in sports. I even relocated for the sole purpose of giving us a new environment, a new school system for him, and a fresh start. I gave him tough love. Yet the tumultuous nature of our relationship persisted.

We had many years of struggle ahead that so many of our friends and family witnessed and tried to help us through. But it wasn't until recently that I realized two things: 1) that going through the tragic loss that we experienced cultivated a certain toughness in both of us. A toughness that wasn't conducive to the proper healing that we needed, nor to strengthening the mother-son bond that we need; and 2) that of all the things that I could do to try to help Kyle, the most impactful thing that he needed all along was not tough love, but rather, tender love. Something as simple as a random hug softens him up like nothing else.

Today, six years later, a lot has changed. My faith is strong, and I've learned a lot. It was definitely a process that took years of tears, praying, fasting, serving, and just choosing to trust God to do a work in my life to get me to the place that I am now. I realize now that having God's protection doesn't mean that I am exempt from the perils of life. But through my pain and seeking God for answers as to why, I understand now that my life's journey is not just for myself, but also for the encouragement of others. Through this journey of healing and restoration, I have relied on two main Scriptures to encourage myself and rebuild my faith. The first is Psalm 34:19, which states, "Many are the afflictions of the righteous, but the Lord delivereth him out of them all," (KJV). The second, and my favorite, is Jeremiah 29:11, which states, "For I know the plans I have for you, declares the Lord, plans to prosper you and not to harm you, plans to give you hope and a future," (NIV). So we will go through things in life, even tragedies for some of us, but God's promise to us is that He will deliver us from all of it, and that even when we have no idea how to cope with today, nor what lies ahead, we can rest assured knowing that God knows and has plans to give us hope for our future.

Those are blessed promises that I relied on to encourage myself to stand up when I was in the deepest despair. I am thankful for the relentless prayers of my friends and family who prayed for us when I wasn't. Eventually, I did start praying again and asked God to give me the strength to make the decision to heal. You see, He had already offered to me His healing, but I did have to make a decision to receive it. And over time, I did just that. I decided I was no longer going to lie in sulk and self-pity nor worry about my future. I decided that I wanted to move forward to create the best life for my family that I could while enjoying it. It was shortly after that God blessed me with a new love, with a wonderful man. And our love story has just begun. I can truly say that I no longer feel discarded, overlooked, or disregarded. I know that I am God's favorite (as are you!), and He has proven to me that He is faithful to perform His promises.

My relationship with Kyle is still progressing day by day. It's not perfect, but we are in counseling and learning to exhibit patience with each other while we heal the damage that was done over the years. I've learned that our relationships with others are what teach us the most about ourselves, and my relationship with Kyle has definitely highlighted some areas for opportunity for improvement in who I am as a mother and as a representation of Christ in the earth. I am learning how to love him tenderly and selflessly. Six years later, God has done a work in us. Our anger has subsided, and we are now at a place of growth and healing, as God continues to show his faithfulness.

My encouragement to you is to stand up! No matter what is going on in your life, you have to find a Scripture that you can lean on that will encourage you through it. Every day may present its challenges, but you can rest assured that God's mercies are new each and every day, and you can make the decision today to exchange your weakness for His strength. This is the strength that I discovered. And this is the strength that you will discover.

PRAYER

Dear Heavenly Father, I thank you for your healing. I thank you for your joy. I thank you for covering us even when we didn't know your plan for our lives. Thank you for your love, your comfort, your peace, and restoration in our lives. Today, I pray that same healing, covering, and comfort for those who are experiencing tragedies or troubles in life. I pray that you would give them a glimpse of the hope that you have for their future, even while they are in the midst of their journey. Lord, I know that we all have different crosses to bear, all for your glory, but I pray that you would provide peace that surpasses all understanding for those who are going through. Your Word says that the prayers of a righteous man availeth much, so I thank you for honoring my prayer today, Heavenly Father. In Jesus' mighty name, Amen.

CHAPTER THIRTEEN

DEEPER WATERS

ALAINA FRANCIS

PRELUDE

From the outside looking in, my story begins with a clubbed foot and people around my parents telling them all of the things in life I'll never be able to do or will fall down doing with or without surgery. Although my human foundation was broken at birth, the strength of my family's spiritual foundation was built up by the preceding generations. Growing up, I always watched my Dad tell close friends and strangers alike about how God healed his infant daughter's foot, how my family, including my older brothers, then three and four years old, would get up every morning and pray while massaging my foot. They would speak the opposite of the doctor's diagnosis over my life and thank God for straightening it, even before it was. I used to wonder why telling the story would end up with my dad, a strong-willed Jamaican, in tears. I'd never experienced anything that forced me to use my foot as an excuse or handicap or caused me to share that part of my story myself. Since I was a newborn at the time, it was my parents who believed for me. While I had yet to understand my own perspective, knowing theirs was enough to help build my faith, and cause a smile to rest on my face with every glance at my straight foot. So, the truth is, my story began with a gift of undeniable evidence of hope in exchange for worry and deep footsteps of faith traced by my parents. However, the understanding and wonder of it all didn't truly begin to sink in for me until the middle of my 21st year.

...

Near the end of 2015, I was in between continuing at my current community college and transferring to another college or university. I had started studying accounting so I could help with our family businesses. But by the end of that fall semester, the timing of an accounting degree wasn't making much sense while my passion for music was simmering on the side. Looking back to when I was about nine, I remember my aunt, a choir director, asking what each choir member wanted to do when we grew up. I loved singing and didn't have stage fright. I just didn't like the spotlight.

So, not being sure what it was called at the time, I said, "I wanted to be the one who puts the music together."

By the age of 21 I had gained more interests. I loved to mentor kids and had a growing curiosity in computer graphics. Though the spotlight remained a signal to run, I still always enjoyed singing with my family at our gatherings. If anyone asked me what I wanted to do as a career, my answer was still music production. But when I realized that all the while I had been writing for more hours a day than sleeping, my answer slowly turned into: "I'm not sure." Ever since learning how to write, I've written to document events in my life's story and to remember dreams. As a teenager, not only was I still writing for fun, but I started writing my journal entries like letters to God. This became another way to pray when my mouth was sealed shut and my head was swirling with overwhelming emotions and anxiety that I would try to hide away. I found it cleared the fog for me to think and hear God more clearly and became my way to release. This quickly turned into filling notebook after notebook that I didn't know what to do with. It was like looking at a labyrinth of paths in front of me. I didn't know which direction to start.

On December 12, 2015, I fell asleep in the middle of the day. I was only asleep for a little more than 20 minutes, but my dream was the kind that stays with you vividly even with eyes wide open.

Journal Entry (12/12/15)

"I was walking in church through the unusual front entrance with my little cousins, 4 and 8 years old, in front of me. Inside, the Pastor's wife was holding the sanctuary doors open; this was also unusual. In reality, I would always greet the pastors in passing with love and respect, but if possible, try to avoid the crowd that usually surrounds them, so I wouldn't be in the way. But in my dream, the crowd was the only way in. While we passed the Pastor's wife, she was talking to someone else, but held her arm out to hug me, so I hugged her. She cut off her conversation and said to me 'Come let me hug you... I can see your heart; you really love children, don't you?' My eyes were closed as I listened to her. She kind of had me smothered like an auntie. I thought 'yes I do'. I then saw myself in what felt like another country helping the kids. I remember all of the bright colors of fabrics, and the sandy shade of the stone ground. I remember the smiles and then I found myself praying in my dream 'Thanking God for everything He's already done, for what's going to happen, and what has already taken place that will affect what's about to take place...' I thought about the big picture again and said in my dream "because it's all about You" Still dreaming I began to hear someone teaching about the meaning of the song "Heart of Worship" and then a piece of the song began playing over and over 'It's all about You. It's all about You Jesus' until I woke up."

I always knew I wanted to travel to help others in some hands-on way when I got older, after college sometime, so I looked at the dream as a reminder of a distant future. But it also felt like another goal that I didn't know the path to reaching. As 2016 started, I convinced my parents to let me have a semester off so I could figure out a direction and start again in the summer. I spent the first couple of months of the year just enjoying the break before I started writing my goals and a plan to reach them. By May, near the end of my break while researching different colleges, I found myself wide-awake in the middle of the dream from five months prior. This was the billboard-sized sign in the middle of the road that helped me understand the connection and power of "writing the vision and making it plain," (Habakkuk 2:2).

My little four-year-old cousin had recently been traumatized causing him to suddenly be terrified of stages. Which meant a very tearful morning with me trying to comfort him while his mom sang on stage and convince him everything was okay before he too had to sing in a choir with his big brother. I gave up convincing him and let him choose. The last five minutes, he decided he wanted to join his brother. When the kids came out to sing, and I saw my little cousin who had just been crying from fear for an hour, singing all of the words and doing all of the actions with a huge smile on his face, I wanted to cry myself. I couldn't be prouder or more relieved! After that rollercoaster of a morning, his mom decided to take him to the line for the pastor to pray for him. I went with her for support but lagged behind when it was their turn. The pastor's wife's assistant was a woman I'd only seen maybe twice before in person, out of the eight years we had been members at that church. She was usually in a different building. We said "Hi," and then she asked if I was okay, which I found a bit strange since not many people can see behind a stranger's smile. I nodded, still smiling. I was fine, just thinking about my little cousin.

Maybe it showed. While the pastor greeted my cousin, the pastor's wife called me up from the back.

She held her arm out to me and said, "Come give me a hug. I saw you. This girl was standing up over there so proud like they were her own children! Yeah, I saw you over there..."

Deja vu?

The next week at church the same pastor's assistant was around again. This time when we greeted each other it felt like either she wanted to say something to me or I was supposed to talk to her for some reason. As I was leaving the building, I walked past the table she was in front of. With the crowd gone, I was able to see it was set up for international missionary work. She told me about a mission trip to Peru the church was taking near the end of summer and asked for my information to send emails and call me about it. I thought, "Ha, not this summer," but gave her my info anyway to keep in contact for a future trip. When I got home and told my mother, her first response was my last guess from her.

"I'll help you go!!" she blurted out before I could even ask or say I wanted to!

But she knew I've wanted to go since I was four years old. Still, my jaw hung there on the floor as she went on listing ideas on how to raise the money. I wondered if she heard me say the trip was *this* summer. I had never in my life been anywhere without at least one other person in my family. They are my comfort, my solid ground! I did not expect my mother to jump right in instantly to be my first sponsor! She usually insisted one of my brothers go anywhere with me.

Hoping she'd take more time to think it through, I asked "Mother, you would send me away just like that?"

"Yeah!" she answered too quickly, like she thought it through long ago and was waiting for the day I'd ask. "It would be really good for you to go."

It was getting too real and happening way faster than I expected. How did we go from a casual conversation on how my day went to me looking at flying over 4,000 miles to another continent? Alone! Yes, I would be with the church team, but no one in my family. What happened to making a plan to continue school? I went to bed stressed, only to wake up to my oldest brother calling from California saying there's a job opening for me at a studio there.

When Mother replied, "Alaina's about to start school," the day after she told me to leave the country in the same summer.

I became even more stressed. What was I supposed to do? I was completely lost in the labyrinth now. The only way to see was to return to my foundation. I had to write. I did nothing but write that entire next day. I didn't eat or even leave the house...just pouring water and tea down my throat while pouring my brain onto the pages. Only then was the connection made between the kids I saw in my dream and the woman in charge of international missions. The pastor's assistant that I'd never met until the pastor's wife said in essence what I heard her say in my dream five months before. A dream, born from the desire of four-year-old Alaina, that I hadn't told anyone but my notebook that never left my side. Suddenly, I knew I had to go. When things start lining up with the Word of God and falling into place and there's peace instead of confusion, I consider it the right direction. So, when an otherwise unexplainable calming joy replaced the seemingly carnivorous butterflies that had been eating away at my stomach for the past two days, it was confirmation. Over the next two months, I watched how everything else lined up. For example, all of the people on the team were from different areas and/or locations of the church but meshed without conflict. All of the roommates, several of us who've only met in the mission meetings, were perfectly matched. And then, a walk-through devotional that the team was given to read daily before the trip talked about how some people might experience what Paul did in Acts 16:9-10, "That night Paul had a dream: A Macedonian stood on the far shore and called across the sea, 'Come over to Macedonia and help us!' The dream gave Paul his map. We went to work at once getting things ready to cross over to Macedonia. All the pieces had come together..."

While preparing for the trip, I was becoming more attached to my guitar and told my mom I wanted to ask the team leader if I could bring it since we were supposed to sing school songs with the kids. Beyond that, it was like a family member I could pack in a bag.

However, I was not prepared for the following statement from mother in the car, "I'll help you create worship sets."

"Huh?" I responded; eyes wide at the idea of being dragged out of my beloved background comfort zone.

Sure, I had gotten more serious about the guitar, and sure, I started singing when I was young, but I'd never sung without the surrounding support of my family's voices or presence. Besides, leading people in worship is totally different from having a few 15 second solos in choir as a kid. My mom knew that though. She started leading in her father's, the bishop's, church as a child and was also one of the main worship leaders in our church at the time. But I kept searching for something; anything to say that would excuse me.

"Mother, I'm not you. I'm not ready for that! I'm not even good enough!" I expressed.

Truth was, I didn't think I was worthy of leading. I was terrified. Not of singing in front of people, but of not knowing if I could direct their focus on what I was singing about instead of me.

"I'm better at following!" I continued.

"Good, follow God. You are good enough and you'll practice. You'll be fine," mother replied.

Having her tell me I would be fine, was as comforting as a professional surfer who already trusted their board on the waves, telling a newbie who had only held her board with feet still on the shore, to just start paddling into the water. But as terrified as I was, I couldn't keep running. At the next meeting I asked our team leader about bringing my guitar.

Her response, "Yes!! You'll be our worship leader!" was confirmation for mother, but I wonder if she noticed the deer-in-headlights feeling behind my smile that time. On the way home from the meeting, mother started listing songs.

Before I could think of another excuse, I heard the ringing reminder in my head of God saying, "And who do you think made the human mouth?" (Exodus 4:11), and I surrendered. I was in the thick of the unknown, but I surrendered. After that, I spent every waking moment hidden away with Jesus, studying, and practicing.

Conversations with my dad about the trip took another inevitable turn on this uncharted route.

When I shared with him that each person on the team was supposed to choose a day to lead a morning devotional, my dad said, "You can share your testimony."

This was the first time it was my turn to share the testimony of my healed foot. I asked my Dad to tell me what happened in detail again. As he went through his memories, he was all smiles, but I heard it differently for the first time. Back in my room, I stared at my straight feet and found myself crying. I couldn't choke out anything but, "Thank You God," past the tears. The next instructions I heard clearly, and I followed without resistance. I made copies of the few baby pictures of me with the short term cast I had on then emailed the team leader asking her to schedule me to share on day seven, the morning when we were going to see the handicapped and special needs children. I wrote out my talking points for my devotional to remind the team that even for people who have yet to experience what God is able and willing to do, we can believe for them and speak the best for their lives and do what we can to help them, like my parents spoke for me before I knew how, and to encourage them to see those children as well-able with God, instead of disabled, as well as the pre-chorus of the song "Alive" by Hillsong Young and Free, translated in Spanish too, for everyone to sing together.

I had no idea that as soon as the door opened to the special needs building, the first little girl I saw, front and center, would have feet like the one I was born with. There was a heavy atmosphere of expectation from everyone in there, the kids, their parents, and our team. As our team began to pray, I began playing my guitar and it was instantly clear that worship for those kids and their parents was simply real. I didn't have to learn a show or fancy words. It was the same as singing to God in my room, and how I always saw my mother prepare to lead, but inviting others to join in. It was a room full of hearts focused on loving the One who loves us no matter what. Every corner of the room erupted with joy and awe. And from that, with a town of witnesses, miracles happened before our eyes. The truth of the Scripture Matthew 19:26 engraved on my mission roommate/dear friend's bracelet rang loud and continued to echo all throughout the trip, "With God, all things are possible."

I couldn't have pictured back then that the one thing I was running from would cause everything I had a passion for to connect, teaching me to lean on God myself while expanding my family with lifelong friendships. When I let go of my plan of picking one of my paths to follow and just surrendered, God washed the labyrinth walls away. Everything I desired to do was found in trusting Him. And so, I am learning to listen ever more deeply to Jesus' whisper. I long for the ripples and waves of the waters He has completely charted. I realize, not only does God give you the desires of your heart, but He will give you what your heart will desire.

"Although sometimes we feel like
We're sinking under the waves,
Or are trapped and lost in a maze,
The truth doesn't change

The unknowns we face are never unknown
To our lives' Savior
Therefore, my prayer remains
Jesus, take me deeper"

CHAPTER FOURTEEN

LOSING THE WEIGHT NOT THE BATTLE

SAFARI CHARLES

PRELUDE

A famous Henry Ford quote states, "Whether you think you can, or you think you can't – you're right." This emphasizes how much attitude determines success or failure.

Childhood

Choices we make as adults are often fueled by obstacles we faced as children. During a pivotal point in my life, I made a decision to cut the cords of the past that held me hostage to being overweight.

I cannot remember a time when I did not battle with my weight. I was overweight throughout grade school and high school. I grew up in Battle Creek Michigan—Cereal City, with my teenage mother and older brother. My mother worked hard to provide for us, but we were still living in poverty. We survived on welfare and food stamps, and my mother only went grocery shopping monthly. We purchased mostly unhealthy foods. Perhaps her reasons behind her food choices might have been due to her upbringing as well as the cost of unhealthy foods and snacks since they were cheaper than the healthy food options, like fruit and vegetables.

Once we ran out of food. Until the food stamps were replenished, we ate what we had left. That often meant eating foods that were high in fat, carbs, sugar, and everything else unhealthy. I recall eating miracle whip and sugar sandwiches, grilled cheese sandwiches, mush, which is cornmeal, hot water, butter, and sugar, and bread balls. I would go to the kitchen, get a slice of bread, and roll it in the palm of my hands until I had perfect bread balls. I ate them non-stop and didn't think anything of it. I don't recall anyone educating me on nutrition or my personal health. Now looking back, I realize that I unknowingly created a binge eating mentality. I ate food like there was no tomorrow because tomorrow, there could be no food.

Ultimately, I followed in my mother's footsteps and also became a teenage mother. I was 16 years old and weighed 190 pounds when I got pregnant with my first son. I tipped the scale at 202 pounds when I delivered. I married my high-school-sweetheart when I was 21 years old. We had three additional children. After the birth of our first child, I lost all of my pregnancy weight without a problem. I thought the same would happen with the delivery of our subsequent children...not so much. I gained over sixty pounds with my second son and only dropped twenty pounds post-partum.

Soon after getting married, I inevitability passed along my bad eating habits to my family. Thankfully, we were not living in poverty, but I still had a poverty mindset. I did not want to spend the extra money on healthier options such as chicken breast or salmon because I could buy twice as much ground beef and chicken thighs or wings for less. I bought tons of chips, fruit snacks, juice boxes, cakes, cookies, and sugary cereal. You name it. My favorite foods to cook were fried chicken, mac and cheese, lasagna, mashed potatoes, meatloaf, spaghetti, tacos, pork chops, and roast beef. My family happily ate every bite.

Lucky for me, my family did not have the same unhealthy relationship with food that I had. My boys were athletes and lived very active lives. I swear my husband was born fit. He always supported my weight-loss goals and would lead the initiative of helping all of us stay active. When my daughters were three and four years old, we went to the high school track in our neighborhood to run and walk a few laps and play around. They were racing one another around the track and playing games. I was in the mix, cheering them on, but my husband was the one really racing with the kids. Aly, my four-year-old who was three-and-a-half-feet tall then, wanted to race. I challenged her to a race, but she said, "No," and expressed that she would rather race against her father because he was faster. I laughed and egged her on by telling her that I was going to dust her. We lined up on the starting line, I with my game face on was ready to run my hardest. "On your mark, get set, go." I took off with my arms pumping and legs moving as fast as I could make them to go, but before we were halfway done with the race, I was left in my four-year-old daughter's dust. I really tried to win, but I couldn't compete...not even a little bit. I laughed it off on the outside. but on the inside, I was really embarrassed and kind of devastated. That eye-opening experience made me face the reality that I was overweight and as a result could not do all of the things that I wanted to be able to do.

Living Overweight

There was one thing that really made me uncomfortable with my being overweight—feeling fat. Anyone who has struggled with their weight knows exactly what I'm talking about. It is that sluggish feeling that you always feel that shortness of breath when you are trying to walk and hold a conversation, or that awkwardness when you have to hold in your breath and struggle to bend over to tie your own shoelaces.

As a Realtor, I would decide which part of the house to show first because of my weight. If we started in the basement, I would have to go from the lower level to the upper level and try not to sound winded by the time we reached the top floor. I would take slow, deep, quiet breaths off in a corner. I did everything I could trying to catch my breath, before resuming our conversation.

Flying on airplanes was extremely uncomfortable, especially if I ended up in the middle seat. I once upgraded to first class just so I could be comfortable. Flying already made me uncomfortable, but flying while fat was another level of discomfort.

The Decision To Change

Something had to change! I truly hated my life. I woke up every day depressed, telling myself that today is the day I will lose this weight. There were so many things in my life that I had no control over, but losing weight was one thing that was totally within my control, if I could only find the strength to stick with a plan.

Friday, July 22, 2011 my life changed forever. Every morning on my way into the office, I had a difficult decision to stay focused on my goals or give into temptation. Some mornings the decision was easier than others, but most mornings, including this day, I gave in and turned into the Dunkin Donuts parking lot. **My go-to breakfast spots were McDonald's and Dunkin Donuts because they both are within walking distance from my house.** I remember ordering a sausage, egg, and cheese croissant, blueberry muffin, orange juice, and a diet coke. That was a normal breakfast for me, but thinking about it now, I ate a day's worth of calories in one meal.

After enjoying my breakfast on the go, I arrived at the office. I sat at my desk STUFFED, disgusted, and totally disappointed in myself. Disappointed because of the lack of control when it came to food I often exhibited. I was tired of the same vicious cycle. I was depressed because I was overweight. I was overweight because I ate too much.

I ate too much because I was depressed. Something HAD to change!

I turned on my computer and an advertisement caught my eye—Weight Watchers featuring Jennifer Hudson. Her before and after pictures looked amazing! That was it...I had had enough! I was sick and tired of being sick and tired and Jennifer Hudson's photo **was a huge motivator for me.** I made a decision that I was ready to make a change...NOW! I signed up with Weight Watchers and started tracking my points with my next meal. Why not Monday or even the next day? Who starts a new food plan in the middle of the day on a Friday? I did because my decision was made...and many Mondays and "tomorrows" had long passed me by.

The Journey

I committed to following the plan exactly as designed for **one** week! Let's be honest. I had tried every other diet known to man. What made me think THIS would be any different. However, in hindsight, none of the other plans were anything that I could do for a lifetime without being miserable. Each day, I tracked my points and ate what I wanted, even snacks. When I stepped on the scale a week later to my surprise, I had lost eight pounds. I was HOOKED!!

My plan was to stop chasing the fast weight-loss plans/fads. You know the ones that promised huge losses in short timeframes and the ones I never managed to stick with pass a day. I remember a three-day diet that I tried, and I didn't make it past breakfast. So, I decided that I would try the slow and steady approach. For example, one to two pounds a week; and IT WORKED!! I could not believe it! I actually went on vacation and came home five pounds lighter while eating what I wanted.

I realized I needed structure, but I also needed some level of flexibility. Don't tell me exactly **what** to eat and **when** to eat it, because then I feel stressed, forced, and deprived. It was like I'm missing something and like it was not my choice. I needed a plan that allowed me to make my own decisions but also would help me to understand the concept of moderation. This plan helped me to know when to say when and how to make healthy choices and to help me take control of my life. I was able to go to a restaurant with friends and not feel like I couldn't have something, instead, I chose not to have unhealthy choices.

I lost 67 pounds and went from a size 22 to a size 10. I also started running and ran FOUR marathons. I still can't believe that because I always wanted to run a marathon, but I never thought I would run FOUR. I also completed five triathlons (two sprints, one Olympic Distance, two Half Ironman events – 70.3), 17 Half Marathons and a ton of other races (5k, 5 mile, 10k, 10 miles, 15k). Again, I pinch myself. I can't believe this is MY life! If I can do it...so can you!

How to Start

Make a plan of action: Decide on a method. What approach you will take to lose the weight? You must have a plan of action and stick with it. What works for everyone else may or may not work for you. How will **you** lose the weight? Will you count calories, carbs, points...whatever works for you? Just make sure it is something you can do for life, not just for right now.

Track your food: I can't tell you how many times I've heard someone say, "I haven't eaten ANYTHING today!" I then asked, "NOTHING all day? Well, I explained all that I had eaten, this food, that drink, and this food! Funny how that went from nothing to more than nothing. Every

HARNESSING STRENGTH DURING TIMES OF UNCERTAINTY

bite adds up! Whether you remember eating it, don't consider it really eating or as a meal, it adds up so write it down! Then you can see where you are spending your calories/carbs/points.

I often make a parallel with money and dieting. The first thing you're taught when you begin budgeting money is to keep a journal of your spending for a few days. By doing so, you have a record of how you are spending your money and then can see where you can make changes or cutbacks.

It's the same with dieting and nutrition. Once you are aware of your habits you can see where you can cutback. Once you are aware of how much an item or food cost in calories, points, or carbs you may find you can't afford to eat it or it's too expensive having too many calories, points, or carbs, and you don't want to spend your money, calories on eating that, after all. That's when you make different choices and healthier **alternatives.**

Plan your meals: Before leaving the house, pack your meals/snacks. Look at the restaurant menu before going. Make your selection before you get there. Do not leave anything to chance. By doing this, it reduced the likelihood that I would overeat. When I'm in the office and hungry, I could reach into my bag and eat one of the snacks that I planned for that day. If I knew I was going out to dinner, I would look at the menu ahead of time and find the meal that fit into my daily allowance, which often required that I make different choices for breakfast and lunch to ensure I stayed within my allotted daily points. I would have to make a conscious effort to go off track.

Make Subtle Changes: You don't have to give up all your favorite foods overnight. Make subtle changes. If your goal is to cut out fast-food, start with eating smaller sized fries or replacing the fries with fruit. Before you know it, your desires change, and you won't miss it.

No one could have ever told me I would give up fast food. I started by only eating the sandwiches without the hash browns or fries. Then, I added only grilled or fish sandwiches. As my daily points continued to decrease, I started making healthier choices and eating clean because going to McDonalds was eating up too much of my daily points. I no longer eat from McDonalds, Burger King, or Dunkin Donuts and have ZERO desire to do so.

Don't Quit: This is by far the hardest battle I have ever fought, but also one I refuse to stop fighting. You will have good and bad days, weeks, and months but that does not mean throw in the towel. I refuse to lose or quit! I started this journey at 246 pounds in 2011. I lost 65 pounds and gained it ALL back and seven additional pounds. But you know what, I still did not quit! I dusted myself off, remembered all the lessons that I learned along the way, and started again. The one thing about doing something once is that you know you can do it again. I am now down 45 pounds and well on my way to my goal. If I can do it, YOU can too! Oh, and that little four-year-old is now 14 years old, and she wishes she could keep up with me.

PRAYER

Dear Heavenly Father, we thank you for your love, kindness, and faithfulness. I pray that you would bless the person who is reading this right now. Help them to know they are not alone on their weight-loss journey that you are there with them each and every day...that you will give them the strength and discipline they need to reach their goal. That your mercies are new every day so do not focus on how long the journey will be...focus on getting through this day and the rest shall be added. "Through the Lord's mercies we are not consumed, Because His compassions fail not. They are new every morning; Great is Your faithfulness," (Lamentations 3:22-23).

Help them to keep thinking on good things and remember "I can do all things through Christ who strengthens me," (Philippians 4:13).

CHAPTER FIFTEEN

A LOVE JOURNEY OF ASSURANCE, HEARTACHE, STRENGTH, POWER & TRIUMPH

LOREN JOSEPHINE FERGUSON

PRELUDE

It was September of 1983 in Cleveland, Tennessee, where we met for the first time. Members of the Church of God of Prophecy global body gather yearly, for the General Assembly. Brian Ferguson, a native-born Bahamian and Loren Thomas, based on God's divine plan and timing, paths were about to cross. I was born in London, England to parents of Jamaican descent. Our meeting was orchestrated with God using a dear mutual friend who introduced us.

This trip for me was a meeting of firsts. It was my first time at the General Assembly and the first time where, when looking back, I can see how my life was about to take me on a path that would change it forever. Without anyone's knowledge, save the Holy Spirit and Heaven, these first bits of unfolding could only begin after my parents emigrated from London, England in April of that same year, relocating to Westchester, New York. For me, meeting Mr. Ferguson was pleasant since I found him very easy to speak with. However, for Mr. Ferguson, this was more than a mere meeting. It was destiny!

Reunited

In 1984 my family and I went to the General Assembly. Mutual friends were reunited. Some were from the U.K., including my dear childhood friend Heather Rodney who was my best friend. This common ground became an opportunity for Mr. Ferguson to find me, and he did. We formed a group which led to spending a lot of time together.

He and his Bahamian friend had noticed that something was wrong with the rental vehicle I was driving. They were both concerned for us, being that we were young ladies going back to our hotel at night and because we were also in the deep south, which also increased their concerns. This premise allowed me to begin to see the heart of Brian Ferguson. With that in mind, they escorted us back to our accommodation by driving in front of our car. They were also very careful in giving us wise counsel on promptly going to the rental dealership to rectify the problem with the vehicle. Yes, I started seeing the heart of this man. I started seeing Brian Ferguson.

Paths of Purpose

We are back at the General Assembly, and it is 1985. There's always a buzz of excitement and expectation in the atmosphere there. Mr. Ferguson, being intentional, was on the stairwell ready to engage me in conversation, which lasted about 15 minutes or so. This was evident, as I was getting ready to exit the sanctuary. He said that since our last meeting in 1984, he had purposed in his heart that upon returning to the General Assembly this year, he wanted to spend time with more spiritually minded persons. That afternoon and during the rest of the Assembly, we spent some time together including dinner dates. He started to become more than an acquaintance. He was becoming a friend.

I received a letter from Brian a month after the General Assembly. He stated how happy he was spending quality time with me and that I was the first woman ever to receive this compliment from him. He said he saw in me qualities he was looking for in a wife. Evidently being blown away, I thought this man was crazy. How could he determine this from the short time we spent together? He said he was coming to the U.S. and would be stopping in New York and wanted to visit me. I was a little startled, however, I agreed to see him during his visit. My parents were somewhat concerned when I told them that I had a friend coming to visit me from the Bahamas. I emphasized Brian was just a friend. Upon his arrival, he stayed in Manhattan with his aunt. The day he came to visit me afforded him the opportunity to meet my parents. They were elated! Praying and fasting was paramount. We courted for seven years.

Engagement

Brian and I got engaged on the beautiful island of Nassau, Bahamas, on October 12, 1991. We were celebrated by a host of family and friends from England, the United States, and the Bahamas.

Wedding

Saturday, October 24, 1992, was a day I will never forget. I woke up that morning with my mind completely made up to marry the man who stole my heart, the man of my dreams, Brian Ferguson. I knew my life would never be the same. With a 10-piece jazz band and lead trumpeter Brian Ferguson serenading me before 300 guests, I walked down the aisle of The Shiloh Baptist Church to the song "You're One in a Million". We exchanged our vows and pledged to love and cherish each other for the rest of our lives. The day was complemented with a wonderful reception where friends and families from near and far celebrated us and celebrated with us.

We've Only Just Begun

After a beautiful honeymoon in Canada, the journey in our marriage had begun. Brian flew back to the Bahamas to prepare for me to join him. On December 13, 1992 my husband returned for me and on December 19, 1992, Mr. and Mrs. Brian Ferguson arrived in Nassau, Bahamas, for their Bahamian wedding reception. What a way to start my married life. Christmas in Paradise Island. I was in the Bahamas with the love of my life. My husband and me. His wife by his side. I was truly happy.

Because of employment reasons, Brian was stationed in Exuma in the New Year of January 1993. I joined him shortly after. I was filled with excitement and expectation that would soon deflate somewhat because of the new normal I had to quickly embrace. Because Exuma is a small island in the nest of 700 islands in the Bahamas, the culture was very different from the lifestyle I was used to. For instance, if I needed something at the store, back home it wasn't a problem. I never had to deal with hearing the clerk tell me, "It's coming on the boat on Wednesday." What? Integration was a must.

For me, this was not going to be fun at all. However, over time I adapted. Brian was assigned as an educator at the local high school in Exuma and life became easier as I integrated as a newcomer in the Bahamas. One thing that stood out to me was my husband's love for people. This wasn't one-sided though. People also loved him. He was very well-known. This was not just in Exuma where we lived, but throughout the Bahamas. With the exception of my husband, I didn't know anyone, so I had to have a friendly disposition about myself. Thank God that was not a new normal for me. Over time I was able to establish new friendships where many are still flourishing today.

It's a funny thing when your body begins to show signs of change that you're not used to. When you finally come to grips with what the change is, well, when I came to terms with what the change was, I told my husband. We were both ecstatic. Yes, we were pregnant! We were going to have a baby, and upon informing both our parents and other friends and families, they too were excited for us. On September 30, 1994, Bradley Kendrick Hylton was born weighing seven pounds and five ounces. Our beautiful first-born son was his father's crown and his mother's glory.

The Smell of Baking

Smells can be interesting, especially the ones that turn you off immediately. This is what I was experiencing but couldn't understand why. There were also moments of not feeling well. What's worse is that we were on vacation in Florida. Upon further investigation, what was causing me to be turned off of certain smells was due to what, as they termed it, was "baking in the oven". Of course, there was excitement once again towards my second pregnancy with high hopes for a girl. Somehow with this pregnancy I was big and there were concerns. However, God was faithful and on March 31, 1998, Leonardo Laurence Jerome came into the world at ten pounds and seven and a half ounces. Bradley was three and a half years old. Motherhood is not just a blessing. It's a gift, I embrace and cherish even to this day.

Well, life adjusted for the Fergusons. Between work, church, the children in school, and babysitters, we met every change with strength and endurance by the grace of God. Love saturated our journey since God taught us how to use it to pave our way through. We did. My husband Brian being the high priest of our home was very careful to ensure that prayer and the Word of God was used to spiritually maintain and sustain our home. No decision was made outside of God's direction. So, as time unfolded, I learned to trust my husband's counsel and judgment. Something was about to happen which would take some time to understand.

The Oil in my Alabaster Box is Costly

The morning of August 6, 2011 was an unusual morning for my husband, Brian and I. We did our morning devotions, which was routine. However, that morning he was very expressive in speaking about his dreams and aspirations. I shared mine as well.

Our worship continued in songs and prayer when Brian said, "I feel strange!"

He stopped talking and his eyes were closed. I couldn't get anything else from him, and then he started foaming. I grabbed the phone, but I also grabbed the olive oil. I wasn't getting any response, so I kept on calling on the name of Jesus. His feet were getting cold and I couldn't get a heartbeat either. I started to anoint him while calling on Jesus and suddenly Brian coughed. I was in shock, while in my heart I was thanking God.

As Brian came out of what we later described as an encounter, his first words to me were, "Baby you prayed me back to life...I was gone."

Tell Me Why the Road Turned

What do you do when life presents a situation that makes no sense at all? Even though Brian regained consciousness, we still went to the hospital. By now Brian was admitted 12 hours ago and he had suffered two seizures, and they were running tests to determine the cause. Besides making calls for prayers, I never left my husband's side. He told me loved me. He told me that he was glad I was his wife.

Upon hearing that Brian was in the hospital, people flooded in, creating excitement everywhere while the medical team hurried to tend to an urgent situation. I met with the doctor about my husband's condition.

"Mrs. Ferguson, I'm so sorry! We tried for an hour, but your husband is gone."

Suddenly, I was walking under water. I couldn't breathe. I had no voice. What I didn't know and couldn't bring to terms was he was not going to wake up. Brian! Brian! Wake up! I wanted him to wake up. I couldn't though since I wasn't dreaming. How do you wrap something like this around your mind? I wanted to hear, even after leaving, "Mrs. Ferguson come back. Your husband is breathing again." This was real and Brian, my beloved of 19 years, took the road that turned. He fell into a sweet sleep at 12 noon on Sunday August 7, 2011.

Hide me now
Under Your wings
Cover me
Within Your mighty hand

When the oceans rise and thunders roar
I will soar with You above the storm
Father, You are King over the flood
I will be still, know You are God

Find rest my soul
In Christ alone
Know His power
In quietness and trust

~Rueben Morgan. Hillsong

Oh, How the Heavens Cried

Brian Kendrick Ferguson! As an educator, a reserve police officer, this man loved and served his community for years. Only 48 years old. His community who also loved him gathered with mixed emotions for his celebration of life, a state-like funeral, his home going. Yet, the whole thing just didn't feel real. Not to mention, that the day was a very somber one. I was smiling on the outside, however, on the inside there was silence, pain, anger, need, bleeding, love, silence. If I looked lost it was because I was. Coming out of the hearse at the church and being escorted down the aisles between two officers, with all eyes on me, was tough. I didn't really walk, I was carried. The Bible says that the Lord is close to the broken-hearted. Paraphrased, He cries with us. And because of who He is sovereignly, He can show us, even using the elements. It rained so hard that day that even the band men were soaking wet as they marched and played to the graveside. Oh, how the heavens cried.

You and Me Against the World

As I found myself surrounded with my world at my feet and my two children, I realized that in the blink of an eye, I had to exchange my crown I wore too proudly as a wife to wear the crown labeled widow.

How was I going to do that? Added to that I was now a single parent. I'm not a single parent. That title is for women who have children without fathers. How am I going to handle all of this? GOD! As much as I was protected by an overwhelming amount of love and support, I felt unprotected. My safety was gone. I was on my face and I couldn't get up. I didn't want to! GOD!

I didn't realize that I was covered and hidden at the same time. It's in this place I got back strength to start again. We lived with my parents in Atlanta, GA. Bradley had transitioned to school in Atlanta, prior, while Leonardo transitioned and registered for High School in 2012. I had to find a job. Over the next few years, I had to make a decision to trust God. This level of trust calls you to walk on deep waters. I watched how the hand of God navigated mine and my children's lives through many rough waters, bringing us out to safety every time. My son Bradley, now 26, is in the Marines where he's deployed in Japan. My son Leonardo, now 22, is an educator residing in North Carolina. I am an empty nester. Most importantly, I am an overcomer. It's because of the One, my soul loves and longs for. He is Christ—the One with me against the World.

CHAPTER SIXTEEN

A MATTER OF TRUST

CARMEN FRANCIS

PRELUDE

"...The Lord is the everlasting God,
the Creator of all the earth.
He never grows weak or weary.
No one can measure the depths of his understanding.
He gives power to the weak
and strength to the powerless.
Even youths will become weak and tired,
and young men will fall in exhaustion.
But those who trust in the Lord will find new strength..."

~Isaiah 40:28-31

I grew up in a Bahamian bishop and first lady's home—the late Bishop Alpheus and Olive Williams. Both of my parents were preacher's kids of preacher's kids. I am the second youngest of eight children. Our childhood days were spent going to school and coming home to get ready and go to church...every day. God's way of doing things was very interwoven into our lives. And considering all the miracles I have seen in my lifetime thus far, I wouldn't want it any other way. Three that come to mind prove that what we were taught: trust God with everything, was always the best option in any situation. God has shown himself strong every time, without fail.

When I was a teenager, my sister lived across town and had stayed over a little late one night. It was usual and easy for us to hang out; being a close-knit family in a small town. That evening, my sister and I decided to take my older sister and her four children home. We packed ourselves into my dad's big old blue sedan late that night. After we got a couple of miles up the road, my dad's clunky car went kaput right under the stop light at the top of the hill. And to make matters worse, the main streetlight was blown out! Fixing streetlights was not necessarily at the top of the list of things to repair in that area of our small city. It might not have been on the list at all. So, there we were with a car full of women and children stuck at a stop light; vehicle stopped dead and the streetlight out in the dark of night at one o'clock am. Not an ideal situation for us, but perfect for a wrong-place-at-the-wrong-time story to unfold. We tried multiple times to start the car; pumping the gas while trying not to flood it and turning the key, but it wouldn't budge.

After a few minutes of what felt like half an hour, in the shady distance we could see a figure coming straight toward the car. "Oh God what is happening?" I worried. I can't imagine how my little nieces and nephews felt. The figure turned out to be a tall man wearing a uniform from a factory that was on the complete opposite side of town. "How strange," I thought. I wondered why he still had his uniform on, since that particular factory didn't even have a graveyard shift. We all scrambled to lock all the doors, until another problem arose. In my dad's old car, one of the doors just wouldn't lock! The man kept heading straight for us and stopped right in front of the driver's side at my sister's window. My sister reached for the hand-powered roller to crack the window down about an inch; making sure she didn't crack it enough for him to reach his hand inside.

He looked right at her and said in a deep and confident voice, "Pop the hood."

As my frightened sisters whispered, "Jesus!" my thoughts were racing in the back seat.

Here we were in the middle of nowhere and anything could happen. What if he was telling us to pop the hood so he could destroy the car even more; making sure it never starts again and therefore trapping us all. It was pure silence in the car as we turned to look at one another. Though it was so dark, we could barely see each other's faces. My sister slipped her hand down to the lever and popped the hood of the car. The moment the man opened the hood, the streetlight immediately turned on. We looked at each other again, quietly gasping with our eyes open wide. Then we all squirmed in our seats trying to see what he was doing under the hood for all of 30 seconds before he was done.

"Try to start it now," he said.

My sister turned the key, and the car started at once! He closed the hood, turned around, and proceeded to walk back down the street from where he came, as if he walked all the way up the street just to help us. Curious as to which house he came out of, we immediately turned the corner and drove in the direction he walked. We wanted to send a thank you card or some other gesture of gratitude. We looked on the right side. No one. Looked on the left in case he crossed the street. Still no one. He was gone. We couldn't find him anywhere! With seven pairs of eyes looking out of all the windows, you would think someone would see something, but the streets were empty, the houses were asleep, and he was nowhere to be found. It was like he disappeared into thin air.

We said to each other, "That was an angel!"

Whether he was or not, we knew God had sent him.

When I was in my late twenties and married with one son, we still lived in the same small town and was still going to church nearly every day. One sweltering hot summer evening, I pulled up about 10 minutes late for choir rehearsal. It was still scorching hot even at 7:10 pm. I got out of the car and began to walk through the parking lot toward the church doors. As I made my way through the parking lot, I started gasping for air and losing my breath. There was a tight heaviness in my chest, and I was really struggling and panting for air. It felt like I was breathing through a coffee-stirrer straw. It was so hard to breathe. My life actually flashed before my eyes. I thought about my family and my baby boy. What if I collapsed right here and never made it to the door? It felt like every step was taken in slow motion. At last, I made it inside where the air conditioning was on and thought "Whew! That was a close call." I had some relief from that hot and humid walk through the parking lot, but there was no way the heat acted alone in impeding my breathing that evening.

The only one I told about that episode was my husband before I scheduled an appointment with my doctor. When I arrived, she ordered an X-ray and then diagnosed me with a rare lung disease for which there was no cure. She told me she wanted to order a biopsy; when they take sample tissue from my lungs to examine the extent of the disease.

My reflexes from growing up in a faith-filled home got a hold of me and I told her, "God is going to heal me."

She responded nonchalantly, "Yeah, but I want to order a biopsy anyway."

She then made a deal with me, gave me an inhaler, and told me to schedule a follow-up X-ray. In reality, she was only trying to prove that she was right. When I got home and told my husband the diagnosis, we started to face the news and I started crying. A helpless feeling began to overtake me and soon overtook my husband as well. We didn't know what to do. Suddenly, as my husband cried out to God, he rolled over and grabbed me and hugged me tight. While holding me in his arms, he began speaking directly to the disease and telling it what it was going to do; that it was going to leave my body and declared that I was healed in Jesus' name. Shortly thereafter, we returned to the hospital for my second X-ray. We were then dealing with a specialized physician who was to discuss my options. When the X-ray was done, the doctor walked in the room with a puzzled look plastered on his face. We did not know what to expect. He was complaining on the way in and then threw the new X-ray up on the light

"I don't understand this," he said bewildered. "Where is it?" Then he threw the first X-ray up and said, "There it is!" Going back to the new one he said again, "But where is it?" Then pointing back at the first, "There it is! Right there! But where is it?"

He couldn't believe his eyes. I couldn't help but dance right there in my seat.

I looked at him and responded, "God healed me. We trusted God and He did it!"

Another son and a few years later, we had a third bundle of joy, a baby girl. She was so gorgeous. She instantly stole the heart of everyone who saw her. Every nurse fell in love with her and nicknamed her Hair. Born with a headful of beautiful hair, our daughter was also born with severe clubfoot, a birth defect in which her foot was twisted out of shape and position. Our pediatrician told us she may need surgery, but in the meantime, he immediately referred us to a pediatric orthopedist to begin the process of casting. As she grew, she consistently had casting and recasting for months and months. We would take her cast off and take her to the doctor for re-examining, in hopes of preventing a long-term disability.

After more months of casting and recasting, it got to the point when the doctor expressed to us that her foot was not responding to the treatment and referred us to an orthopedic surgeon. The surgeon examined our baby girl and told us to see the receptionist to schedule the surgery for six weeks out. He explained in an effort to correct her foot, he was going to perform a surgical procedure to reposition the tendons and ligaments in the back and better position her foot. After surgery, she would be in a cast for another two months and then may need to wear a brace for a year or more to prevent the clubfoot from returning. He said the surgery might help, but it wasn't guaranteed to work. Our daughter could still have a problem, even after surgery.

Earlier, one of our peers had told us of her niece's experience, who was a young adult, born with the same issue and occasionally falls when trying to run or often stumbles when she walks. Even after hearing her story, we refused to allow fear to drive us.

My husband said to me, "What is the point of scarring our baby for life because we're trying to experiment?"

After the surgeon walked out, while getting our daughter dressed, my husband stopped! He grabbed our daughter's foot and spoke to it just as he spoke to my lungs a few years before. He spoke in authority, directly addressing the issue and told her foot what it was going to do in the name of Jesus. We knew our God was more than able to do "exceedingly, abundantly more than we could ask or think," (Ephesians 3:20). We then proceeded to the receptionist to schedule the appointment. During those six weeks, every morning and each night before bed, he would massage our daughter's foot. As a family, even our young sons, we would thank God for her healing. It wasn't a prayer for healing anymore, since we had already prayed and believed when we prayed. It was now a prayer of thanksgiving, as we trusted God that it was already done. "...when you pray, believe that you receive them, and you will have them," (Mark 11:24).

Six weeks went by, and we took her back to the surgeon. Our daughter was a little over a year old and was beginning to walk by then. We walked in the office and while the doctor was prepared for surgery, we still trusted God to do what He does best—show Himself strong.

"Okay doc," my husband said to the surgeon. "You told us our daughter needed the surgery because of xyz, but look at her now."

"Okay," the surgeon replied, a bit skeptical.

We put our little girl down and told her to walk to the doctor, and we all watched her walk over to him.

Then the doctor said to her, "Okay. Go back to your dad."

My husband called her, and we watched her walk back while the doctor observed. This exchange happened about three times before the doctor picked her up and put her on the examination table. He took the shoe off of the foot he planned to do surgery on and examined it closer.

"Hmm," he said.

Then taking her other shoe off he put both of her feet together.

"Hmm. I see," he continued. "I see what you mean," and he walked out the door and cancelled the surgery.

Everyone needs a reminder to trust God no matter how close you are to Him. It's with these reminders that our faith is strengthened even more. Until this day, we praise our Father God for the miracles He's done in our lives. It will never get old. We will always remember how He came through for us when we trusted Him with our lives; how He stepped in and delivered. If you get nothing else, just know that no matter what you go through, have faith. You can trust God in everything! "...Because anyone who wants to approach God must believe both that he exists and that he cares enough to respond to those who seek him," (Hebrews 11:6).

It's a matter of TRUST!

T • <u>Talk</u> to your Father about everything that concerns you.

R • <u>Rely</u> on Him to speak to you and be willing to obey His voice.

U • <u>Understand</u> that you are His child, and He's got you.

S • <u>Seek</u> Him first in every area of your life, always.

T • <u>Testify</u> or <u>Tell</u> someone about how He came through for you.

CHAPTER SEVENTEEN

THE SEED SOWER

DAWN FRANCIS

Then He spoke many things to them in parables, saying: "Behold, a sower went out to sow. And as he sowed, some seed fell by the wayside; and the birds came and devoured them. Some fell on stony places, where they did not have much earth; and they immediately sprang up because they had no depth of earth. But when the sun was up, they were scorched, and because they had no root they withered away. And some fell among thorns, and the thorns sprang up and choked them. But others fell on good ground and yielded a crop: some a hundredfold, some sixty, some thirty. He who has ears to hear, let him hear!" (Matthew 13:3-9).

My parents sowed many spiritual seeds into our lives. They both considered their children and church members as good ground. I remember once when my dad had come home from work and it was cold and icy outside. It was time for bed, and we knew he had to be up very early for work. As a pastor of a growing church, dad also worked as a full-time carpenter. He would leave before we got up for school, as he had to travel out of town for his work. Nonetheless, whenever there was a need, dad would often come to the rescue. One particular night, he got out of his bed in the middle of the night to go out and assist a neighbor. He heard the sound of a car stuck in the snow and the neighbor having a hard time getting out. The revving noise of the engine must have awakened him. Dad immediately put on his clothes, boots, gloves, and coat and proceeded out with a shovel in hand.

When he came back to the house, we asked him, "Daddy, why did you do that?"

We knew he was tired and needed rest. His response was one I will never forget.

He said, "This is for you all!"

He was sowing a seed that he knew would come forward to his future generations. He had seven girls, of which I am the youngest. I can tell you time and time again that strangers have stopped and given me a helping hand whether to change a tire, give a needed jump-start, pushing my car out of the snow, or simply to say, "Hello ma'am, is everything okay?" Those seeds my daddy sowed back when he was alive are still blooming in my life and my family's lives today. Dad knew that we would go through challenges, so he paved a future to assure our needs would be met by helping others.

We go through life challenges so that we can help others to go through what may be considered their most difficult and desperate seasons: a season of grief, a season of depression, illness, a season of darkness or an indescribable season. Our struggles and triumphs, when shared faithfully, are the inspirations that support others to know there is hope. None of us may fully understand and know where we are at that moment. We have to know that it's okay and that we are not alone nor are we the only one who has endured.

We often feel alone and secluded during our most difficult moments. This is a trick that the enemy of our souls plays on us. Just think about the impact of the added quarantine we are facing here in 2020. Whatever the situations we are going through are being compounded by the sense of isolation and separation we endure daily. But we are not alone. God is with us. The word of God speaks to how God designed us as his children to need one another. We fulfill his plan by sowing seeds into the lives of others and caring for one another.

Social media displays so much on self-care and looking out for oneself. But is it God's choice for our lives? I would adamantly respond, "No!" We talk about self-care and the ways in which we can take better care of ourselves. But the truth of the matter is, as much as we take care of ourselves, we are to help one another. We are to be uplifting and encouraging towards our sisters and brothers.

Life's journey is filled with bumps and potholes along the road. There are smooth paths as well, with beautiful pastures. This is a journey that we are all on together. We need one another to make it. If I can share something to lighten your load, to let you know, I have been there too. Allow me to share that I walked that road, and here are the potholes and bumps to look out for. I can share how you can avoid those dangerous bumps and potholes. You may take heed, or you may decide you want to face those potholes and bumps on your own. But know that there is someone that God has placed in your path to let you know that He is there for you. They are there to affirm that He will never leave or forsake you.

How important is it to give someone support or hope in life? As I think through my days and nights in graduate school, work, and ministry, I realize the words of encouragement from others are what helped me to take step after step. There were times when I couldn't clearly see the steps that I needed to take. But in my younger years, I had a family who directed and encouraged me to go after my dreams and goals. No matter the goal, I was encouraged to trust God and see it through.

Countless times I recall feeling lost and alone, perplexed about making the right decisions. I know that I wasn't alone because I know the word of God says He will never leave us nor forsake us. Trusting in the Word helped to carry me through the struggle. At times, I sensed an isolation that was nearly indescribable and filled with intense pain. The enemy, satan, likes to isolate us so that he can use his tactics to bear down on us. The enemy's desire is for us to lose sight that our Creator is carrying us through the storm, trial, pain, or season and bringing us faithfully into victory.

Why? I used to hear trials come to make you strong. I thought, "What if I don't want to be strong?" Family, friends, and coworkers often say how strong I am. Trust me, it's not always what I was feeling. Sometimes I felt as though I was barely standing. Other times I wondered how I was even able to continue standing. But I know that God was always with me. He will always be with you too. So, it's about sowing good seeds. It's about helping those who are in need when we can on this journey. It's about lending a hand to pull up our sister or brother. This is a song from my dad's generation, but it reflects a message that needs to be shared today. Mahalia Jackson, the famous singer, wrote these words that sum it up.

> "If I can help somebody, as I travel along
> If I can help somebody, with a word or song
> If I can help somebody, from doing wrong
> No, my living shall not be in vain.
> No, my living shall not be in vain.
> No, my living shall not be in vain.
> If I can help somebody, as I'm singing the song
> You know, my living shall not be in vain."

~ Mahalia Jackson, "If I Can Help Somebody"

All of us want to sow seeds and reap a harvest that is bountiful, beautiful, productive, and impactful for future generations. We want our living to be what some would call a legacy. We want to help those who we can by sharing, building up, encouraging, and by inspiring people to understand that they are not alone. Share your wisdom by speaking and declaring God's word into the lives that you are designed by the Creator to impact. Hebrews 13:5: "I will never leave thee, nor forsake thee."

PRAYER

Father God, I thank you for carrying me through every trial. Thank you for giving me the strength to endure and triumph over every situation.

Thank you for your word, your promises, and your faithfulness. I pray that I will continue to have the courage to bless others by sharing with those in my path. I declare and decree blessing and strength over myself now and others, in Jesus' name. Amen.

Published by: Life Legacy Publishing

Graphic Design: Karen Bowlding

Cover Design: Brittanye Williams

ISBN: 978-1-7363120-0-1

Printed in the United States

DEDICATION

This book is dedicated to the parents and loved ones of each writer; our champions who encouraged us and sacrificed to make our lives better. Thank you for your love and support. Our goal is to keep your legacy alive as we bless and encourage others through life's journey.

FOREWORD

It is an absolute honor for me to write this foreword for Dawn Francis about a topic that is so important to the body of Christ, and people world-wide. Each of us must come to a place where we discover the strength of God, and harness that strength during times that appear to be uncertain. Although we will face challenges, the fight doesn't have to be hard and unbearable. While going through challenges typically reveals what is in us, I am confident that with the wisdom and tools that are shared throughout this book, by the myriad of gifted writers, will equip you, and motivate you to maximize the seasons that you are in. As you partner with the Holy Spirit to discover God's strength within you, you too can experience the miraculous healing and victory, God preordained for you to experience in every area of your life. I thank God for Dawn and her heart to serve others by penning a powerful, impactful, and life changing book.

Dr. DeeDee Freeman, First Lady
Spirit of Faith Christian Center

INTRODUCTION

As readers, we search for ways to gain knowledge, sometimes to escape reality, and other times simply for fun and enjoyment. This is a book that I hope will do that and more. I have asked several of my gifted friends and family members to share with you their personal stories of STRENGTH, TRIUMPH, AND VICTORY; stories that have marked change in their lives and ministry. I know that this book will be beneficial and a life changing blessing to everyone who decides to take a peek into their lives.

Everyone experiences life's changes and struggles that can bring out that feeling of "I don't know how I am going to make it!" and cause questions such as "How will I keep my sanity through this?" Whether it be the loss of an opportunity, losing ourselves, or the devastating losses of loved ones at some point in our lives, the destabilizing anxiety that comes with uncertainty can feel as though it just might take you out... and it resonates with us all.

Through these stories of "Discovering Strength: Harnessing Strength During Times of Uncertainty" we recognize that during these uncertain seasons in life while it seems that we can't find the strength to go on, we will in fact make it across to the other side. When we see how far we've come, we realize that we did have the power to endure and one step at a time, we find that it is nothing but the unmerited favor of God carrying us through it all.

CONTENTS

ABOUT THE AUTHORS

 **DAWN RENEE FRANCIS**, a woman of faith, launched her educational journey from the prestigious Peabody Conservatory of Music, from which she attained a Master of Music Degree in Vocal Performance. Continuing in the educational realm, Dawn embarked on her professional music journey as a teacher in the Michigan Public School System and later the Greater Washington D.C. area --spanning elementary, middle, and high school and college education levels for over 20 years, specializing in Music Education.

Equally gifted as a professional singer, Ms. Francis' soloist performance on "Wait on the Lord", reached #8 on the Billboard Charts. Her vast repertoire spans classical opera and art song, gospel, and jazz, while her performances have extended throughout North America, Europe, and South Africa.

Complementing her musical accomplishments, Ms. Francis continues to enhance and inspire others as a vocal trainer, choral director, worship leader, and an opera/musical theater actress with her powerful Spinto Soprano voice. In addition, she faithfully served as the Director of the Music Ministry at several churches; zestfully working to fulfill her purpose and destiny, catapulting ministries and musicians to the next level of excellence in the Kingdom of God.

SEAN SIMMONS, is the father of two young boys. Currently residing on the East Coast in Silver Spring, Maryland. He co-authored a very well written book called "this book". He has practiced a great deal in the past with writing comedy, joke writing, short stories, music, and improv sketch comedy. In the past, his creative  writing experience has proved him to be a dedicated professional, a hard worker, and a quick study. Sean desires to impact the human situation through comedy, laughter, and hope. His deep faith provides him with a center-focus on improving lives and seeing people overcome trauma and situations through comedic relief.

 **THELMA J. HAYES** is a wife, mother, minister, mentor, teacher, advisor, and friend! I am married to the love of my life, Carl Hayes, for 36 years. Together, we have two adult daughters and one handsome grandson. God has allowed me to serve as a missionary to Mexico, Haiti, Zimbabwe, the UK, and Canada. Teaching is my passion, no matter the topic. Whether biblical teaching or math and English, I enjoy teaching individuals of all ages. I hold a Master of Science in Education and am currently pursuing my doctorate in Special

Education. Together, my husband and I serve in our local church, Hope Christian Church, Beltsville, MD, as leaders, small group ministers, and children's ministry.

I enjoy reading, writing, and mentoring teens and adults. Several years ago, I started a group, U R Unique Leadership, to encourage positive relationships between mothers and daughters. Jeremiah 29:11 reminds me that God has good plans for me. As I share from my heart the many blessings that God has given me through writing, I believe lives will be touched and transformed for kingdom purposes. We have a strength that goes well beyond ourselves; that strength is in Jesus Christ. Journey with me through remarkable life adventures crafted by the hand of the Father to glorious victories which proclaim His sovereign love!

CEOLA CHARLES is a God-fearing woman who is a native of the beautiful Island of Nassau, Bahamas. She worked in banking for 20+ years, while also maintaining a part-time career as a cosmetologist, just because she loves serving people. Ceola discovered that her main passion is to encourage people through warm,  compassionate listening, and words of faith. While she has had several major goals in life that she has achieved, and others she is in pursuit of, she is happy to now pronounce herself as a published Author. Ceola is very family oriented, having four children and 12 grandchildren, currently. For fun and relaxation, Ceola enjoys family gatherings and cooking meals for her family. God has truly blessed her with enduring strength throughout the years, and she is excited to share a part of her story with readers.

VALERIA C. LATIMORE was born and raised in Battle Creek, MI, also known as the Cereal City. She is a Minister of the gospel, mother of two daughters, mentor to young women, business coach and entrepreneur for over thirty years. Valeria currently owns a full-service salon, distribution company, advanced training school for barber and beauty professionals, and coaching network for business owners. In the near future Valeria plans to open a home for teenage mothers equipped with counseling for the mothers as well as for teenage fathers to teach them how to have a healthy relationship with each other so that they can properly raise a child to be a productive citizen in a healthy environment. Valeria has many goals and plans on the horizon that's going to promote wealth and health, not only in her family but in everyone that she encounters.

ADRIENNE VARLACK began her faith journey at the age of nine and has continued on with the Lord ever since. She has filled several leadership positions within the church and has provided family and marriage counseling alongside her husband, to whom she has been married for 28 years. Adrienne served as the Director for the Pregnancy Testing Center in Mission, TX, counseling expectant mothers for six years and providing student education in public schools during that time. After the death of her youngest child, she combined her passion for healthcare awareness and her 40 years of business acumen and pursued a Bachelor of Healthcare Administration from South Texas College in 2014. She intends to continue her education with a Masters in Family Counseling, specializing in Grief Counseling.

KATRINA PORTES is a native of the cereal city, Battle Creek, MI. Having spent her youth there, she later relocated to the East Coast to attend the University of Maryland, College Park (Go Terps!!), where she earned her Bachelor of Arts Degree in English. She subsequently attended the University of Maryland, University College, where she was conferred a Master of Science in Technology Management, and an MBA. Katrina attends Spirit of Faith Christian Center, where she serves on the praise team, under the pastoral leadership of Drs. Michael and Dee Dee Freeman. When she is not serving her Real Estate clients, you can find Katrina spending quality time with her beautiful family.

ALAINA I. FRANCIS is a singer, writer, musician, and music producer with a deeply rooted passion for God, her family, and culture. She has been singing for most of her life, is a self-taught guitarist from the age of 18, and enjoys many expressions of writing; from poetry, lyrics, and melodies,  to fictional stories and journaling. Alaina is inspired by art in every sense of the word and dedicates her time to pouring into the next generation to help them grow as those before her have done for her.

DONNA MAZYCK has been a nurse in community settings for most of her career. She worked as a school nurse in high school and alternative school settings. Donna worked in state governments and currently works as an association executive. She  advocates for the health and wholeness of all people. Donna uses her words to encourage people. She enjoys long walks, meaningful conversations, and time with family and friends. Donna is married to her college sweetheart. They have three adult children and one grandchild. Donna found purpose in life when she began her journey as a Christ-follower in her teens.

PAULINE VIOLET REID is a native of Nassau Bahamas. With her passion for music ministry, she has traveled internationally as a powerful, anointed, and dedicated director for choirs of all ages. She is also the First Lady of Wildwood COGOP in Cleveland, TN, where she serves as the praise & worship leader, and Women's Ministry Director. Pauline is a Pastor's wife and a mother to many. She finds delight in writing her first book and trusts that you'll be blessed and encouraged.

ORDEAN SIMMONS, was born and raised in Toronto Ontario Canada. Ordean is the daughter to Orville and Phyllis Clarke, sister to Shantel Clarke, wife to Bjorn Simmons, and mother to their two beautiful children Olivia and Liam.

With having a love for travel at an early age, Ordean has seen parts of the Caribbean, UK, France, Italy, and Mexico with her friends and family. She hopes to one day make a journey to the continent of Africa with family and friends.

Now living in Maryland, Ordean works as a Project and Risk Manager with experience in hospitality, events, and vendor management. Her career encompasses mentoring, training and development, people management, and philanthropic endeavors with various community leaders with a Top 30 under 30 award for her contributions as a leader in the hospitality industry.

Thankful for the anchors in her life that never let go, Ordean continues to give back to those who may feel they have been forgotten. She has made it a mission to be someone else's anchor and has plans to write her first children's book in the coming year.

LINDA P. WILLIAMS, IT Strategic Professional, Realtor, Entrepreneur, and Author, graduated from Michigan State University with a Bachelor of Art (BA) in Psychology and Math. Linda has leveraged her technical and strategic planning background to all aspects of her 25+ year professional career. As a Project Management Professional (PMP) and Certified Scrum Master (CSM), Ms. Williams' acumen for process improvement permeates both business and personal endeavors, as well as her passion for mentoring and training, both youth and adults. Linda is happily married to her husband, Winston, and is the mother of one daughter, Brittanye.

SAFARI CHARLES is a 44-year-old wife of 22 years, mother of 4 amazing children, child of God, and Realtor. Motivated by her desire to be an example to her daughters, she lost 65 pounds.

Her journey started with fitness, running 5-6 days a week. It wasn't until she changed her eating habits along with working out did she see results. She lost 65 pounds, transforming from a size 22 to a size 10, ran four marathons, 17 Half Marathons, and completed 5 triathlons.

LOREN FERGUSON has been serving in Ministry for over four decades including Director of Women's Ministry now under the leadership of Bishop Lloyd G. Phipps, over the past 6 years, at the Covington Drive Church of God of Prophecy, Decatur, Georgia. She believes it is important for  women to find their purpose in life, thus her passion is encouraging them to do so.

Loren has been widowed for over nine years. Their union was blessed with two beautiful sons (Bradley, United States Marines, and Leonardo, Educator).

Presently, serves at The Good Samaritan Health Center, Atlanta in several capacities including but not limited to the Market Manager. She is also pursuing a Doctorate Degree in Wholistic Counseling. Her first profession was a paralegal.

Loren's Journey has been one of faith and deep trust in God; while loving Him enabling and encouraging her to write while also listening to music.

Loren Ferguson was born in London, England to the union of Hylton and Norma Thomas and has four brothers: Livingston, Alrick, Keith and Kevin.

ERICA BATES is a writer, artist, and educator. She believes that her writing can inspire and empower individuals to live life to the fullest. With over 25 years of classroom experience and an Educational Specialist degree, Erica Bates strives to generate a joy of learning in young people's  lives. She has a Maryland Educator Certificate in Early Childhood Education Pre-K-3 and an Association of Christian Schools International Educator's Certificate for the elementary level. While pursuing her doctorate degree in curriculum and instruction, Erica mentors and serves in her community through various organizations. In addition to writing, Erica enjoys presenting and engaging in local and national education conferences. Erica's goal is to empower educators as they make a positive impact in the lives of their students.

 **CARMEN FRANCIS** is from a small city but has always loved thinking big. She is married to her best friend and they partnered in ministry for years; God blessed their union with three gifted children. After graduating with an IT degree, she continuously found her journey leading in the direction of serving others. Her passion for music, singing, and art was a driving force for many years. Carmen is vocally trained, with 20+ years coaching small vocal

groups and other vocalists. She has a huge heart for God and an instinctive desire to pursue Him and it's that zeal that has kept her aspiring for greatness while training and encouraging others to reach their goals.

CONTACT

https://www.dawn-francis.com

Made in the USA
Middletown, DE
23 February 2021

SEVENTEEN STORIES.
ONE PURPOSE.
STRENGTH & ENCOURAGEMENT.

As readers, we look for ways to gain knowledge, sometimes to escape reality, and other times, simply for fun and enjoyment. In this book, several gifted friends and family members share their stories of STRENGTH, TRIUMPH, AND VICTORY with you. The feelings of, "I don't know how I am going to make it," or "How am I going to get through this situation, and remain sane?" resonates with a lot of us at times. As you take a peek into their life stories and experiences, allow the stories to take you to a place which brings comfort, healing, and encouragement.

In the pages of this book, tremendous stories come to life. These words dance across the page with emotion and transparency, compelling us to take part. We know life. Life brings the unexpected and the power in these stories point us to a place of honesty. Take time to ask the question. What is my story? What has God brought me through? Just as our friends share their stories with you, be inspired to tell your own story. God is not finished writing your book.

ROXANNE CORBETT

This book will encourage and strengthen you when you go through different circumstances in your life. It will help you to be victorious. As you read the stories you can see the hand of God moving on their behalf. Stay in relationship with Him and He will give you the strength to conquer any situation (Isaiah 40:29).

PASTOR BRENDA WILLIAMS

$14.9
ISBN 978-1-7363120-0-
5149

9 781736 312001